NATURALLY
IT'S GOOD

. . . I cooked it myself!

NATURALLY
IT'S GOOD
. . . I cooked it myself!

Robin Toth

BETTERWAY PUBLICATIONS, INC.
White Hall, Virginia

First Printing: March, 1982

Published by Betterway Publications, Inc.
White Hall, VA 22987

Distributed to the book trade by
The Berkshire Traveller Press
Stockbridge, MA 01262

Illustrations by the author
Typography by David Wagner

Library of Congress Cataloging in Publication Data

Toth, Robin H.
    Naturally it's good...I cooked it myself!

    Includes index.
    Summary: Explains how good nutrition contributes to good health and includes more
than 100 simple, nutritious recipes.
    1. Cookery—Juvenile literature.
2. Nutrition—Juvenile literature.   [1. Cookery.   2. Nutrition]   I. Title.
TX652.5.T68   641.5′123   81-21754
ISBN 0-932620-09-4   AACR2

Printed in the United States of America

Dedicated to Joshua and Sarah, my two kids.
Naturally they're good...they're mine!

CONTENTS

Introduction

Remember the first morning you woke up early (before Mom!) and sneaked into the kitchen? Making breakfast all by yourself was an adventure that always tasted good. The best part was not having any adults looking over your shoulder, telling you what to do and how to do it. Second best was realizing that nothing else makes you as self-sufficient as cooking for yourself. This book is dedicated to those memories.

But don't let what you learned then—the good feelings, the "smart" feelings—become only memories. Help yourself grow! Make yourself an expert on your body and how it works, and you will know—better than anyone else—what's good for you. Tickle your tastebuds! Please your palate! But don't stop there; between the first tasty bite of food and the last, there is a whole lot going on!

Although each of us feels special and unique, life itself seems pretty simple. We are born. We eat. We grow. Our bodies take care of themselves, unless attacked by "mysterious" germs.

For some of us it really is that simple. But more and more of us are discovering we have to give thought and consideration to what and how we eat. No longer are we content to pull a package out of the pantry or freezer. Instead, it gives us a good feeling to understand the relationship between what we eat and what we become, and to decide for ourselves what our bodies and minds and emotions need to operate smoothly.

Once you decide *you* want to be in control—after all, you will be living with that body for the rest of your life—you should start with some basic facts. That's where this book tries to help. And don't be too confused if some of these "facts" change as new information becomes available or new opinions are shared with you. If you learn to understand your body, learn to listen to the "doctor" inside you, you will be well on your way to the healthiest life you could possibly have.

Get acquainted with your body. Pay attention to it. Listen to it. Remember, no body can tell you more about your body than *your* body.

The ABC's of Nutrition

Girls and boys, preteens and teenagers, young ladies and gentlemen . . . Step right up! Are you ready to learn the *Facts of Life*? Do you think you are old enough? Well then, turn the page. It's time to begin . . .

The ABC's of Nutrition

Cells form the foundation of life at all levels, ours included. You have more than one hundred trillion cells in your body. 100 trillion! That's 100,000,000,000,000! And they all have to be fed!! Everyone seems to agree on the basic requirements of our cells. We know of forty-five elements, called essential nutrients, that are needed by our cells, but we don't know of any one food—or group of foods—that can supply us with all of these elements at one time.

These are the forty-five essential nutrients we need to live:

45 NUTRIENTS ESSENTIAL TO LIFE

The 8 Essential Amino Acids:
Isoleucine
Leucine
Lysine
Methionine
Phenalalanine
Threonine
Tryptophan
Valine

The Vitamins
A
D
C
E
K
Thiamine
Riboflavin
Niacin
B_6 (pyridoxine)
Folacin
B_{12}
Pantothenic acid
Biotin
Choline

Fatty Acid
Linoleic acid

The Minerals
Calcium
Phosphorus
Magnesium
Sulfur
Sodium
Potassium
Chloride

The Trace Minerals
Iodine
Iron
Copper
Cobalt
Manganese
Zinc
Fluorine
Molybdenum
Selenium
Chromium
Nickel
Tin
Vanadium
Silicon

Nitrogen

Don't be disappointed in yourself if you don't recognize the names of many of these nutrients. Outside of nutritionists and other professionals who work and study in this field, not many people do. Anyway, it isn't important that you know all the names. This is not a test! What is important is that you know what foods provide your body with the nutrients it needs for health and growth.

About twenty-five years ago, nutritionists created a concept they called the **four basic food groups.** (Before then they had used a system of seven basic groups.) They hoped to give average people, who were not scientists, nutritionists, or other health experts, the information they needed to plan healthy and nutritious diets.

Long ago, and this is still true in some countries and cultures, a human being would eat an entire plant or a complete fish—bones, eyes, and all. Eating that way gave that person a much better chance of eating a balanced diet. Today, unfortunately, many people have moved away from farms and coastal villages. In doing that they have moved away from easily available, naturally occurring, balanced diets.

When the group of nutritionists I mentioned before put together the four basic food groups, they did so only after studying carefully what most people ate in our country. Then they divided these most commonly eaten foods into groups, according to which essential nutrients they included. These important food categories have become known as:

THE FOUR BASIC FOOD GROUPS

Group 1: Vegetables and fruits
Group 2: Cereals and baked goods
Group 3: Milk and milk products
Group 4: Meat and meat alternatives

The nutritionists recognized that each of these groups include certain foods which contain certain nutrients. Their basic idea—a good one and easy to follow—is this: If you eat the recommended number of servings from *each* group, *every* day, you will enjoy a balanced diet.

The first group, vegetables and fruits, is really important. Maybe you haven't been too excited about eating your broccoli or spinach, or drinking your orange juice, but you are getting older now. Sure, it's always been your body, but the responsibility for its care and treatment is yours now, more than it ever has been before. Eat those vegetables and fruits. Did you know that we depend on those foods for most of our vitamins and minerals? Much of the fiber we need comes from those foods, too. Because different specific nutrients come from different fruits and vegetables, it would make sense for you to know the best sources before deciding what your four daily servings will be. You'll want to make sure, for example, that one serving is loaded with vitamin A and that another is bursting with vitamin C. Examples of servings? On a typical day you might have an orange, a portion of string beans, a medium-size potato, and a small bowl of cole slaw.

The second basic food group, cereals and baked goods, doesn't just include those crispy flakes you like for breakfast. All the seeds from the grass family—wheat, rye, barley, rice, corn, oats, and buckwheat—belong here. What do we get from these foods? First, and most important, is the energy they provide us. They also have carbohydrates (a major source of energy), the B vitamins, iron, some protein, and more fiber. Your body needs four servings of these foods daily. Tomorrow, you might have a slice of whole wheat toast, a corn muffin, a bowl of rice, and a small plate of noodles or spaghetti.

Milk and milk products, the third group, were chosen for the calcium and phosphorus they provide. Although these foods contain many different vitamins and minerals, calcium and phosphorus are the nutrients of greatest concern to nutritionists. Why? When they studied the kinds of foods Americans were eating on a regular basis, they learned many of us were not eating foods rich enough in those two nutrients. Kids your age—from ten through high school—should be getting three or four servings of calcium-containing food every day (four if you are a teenager). Foods in this group include milk and all the other dairy products; whole milk, buttermilk, yogurt, cottage cheese, and ice cream, for example. For one day's servings you could have milk at breakfast, try a grilled cheese sandwish and a glass of milk for lunch, and maybe yogurt for an after-school snack.

The last group includes meat and meat alternatives. Under this heading we find meat, of course, as well as poultry, fish, eggs, dried beans and peas, and seeds and nuts. What do we get from these foods? Some vitamins and minerals, but they primarily contribute protein and iron to our diets. Everyone needs two servings of 2 to 3 ounces every day. Maybe you'd like tuna salad at lunch and hamburger or pot roast for dinner, maybe a ham sandwich for lunch and chicken for dinner. If you feel like a meatless day, you could satisfy these needs with a bowl of rice and beans at dinner time, and a peanut butter sandwich on whole-wheat bread for lunch.

Well, that's it. Those are the four basic food groups. Are you wondering why foods like butter and candy have not been included? When the experts who put these groups together saw how much fat and sugar we were eating, they decided we were already having more than enough! Most people enjoy a sugary treat now and then (me, too!), but if you are eating a balanced diet you are getting all the sugar and fat your body needs. Some fat is already present in many foods, especially dairy products, nuts and seeds, and animal foods (meats especially).

There are other ways to decide what foods you need to be healthy, but making daily selections from the four basic food groups is one of the easiest to remember. Let's see what else each group has in store for us, starting at the beginning.

Apple to Zucchini; from A to Zinc

Food Group 1: Vegetables and fruits

An apple a day won't really keep the doctor away—not all by itself, anyway—but it will help. Fruits and vegetables are important foods, primarily because of the essential vitamins and minerals they give us. They supply us with plenty of fiber, too; that helps your body produce a healthy kind of bacteria that encourages you to use the vitamins and minerals you digest.

And that isn't all high-powered fruits and vegetables do for you. Besides fiber and nutrients, they also supply a high water content. Water helps carry the vitamins and minerals to our cells. If you eat a meal heavy in salt or meat, vegetables will help to break up the salt and animal fat, making it easier to digest them. Root vegetables like carrots, turnips, and radishes are especially good for this purpose. There are a lot of reasons why you should listen to Mom, and **eat your vegetables!**

Many people have learned they can more easily digest fruits that grow in the area or country in which they live. The fruits we are most likely *not* to digest comfortably or to be allergic to are those grown in a tropical climate. Citrus fruits, pineapples, mangoes, and coconut are high on the list of troublesome foods for some who have food allergies and other digestive problems.

Here is a list of all the different kinds of fruit you eat now or are likely to eat in the future, with a brief description of the nutrients each fruit provides. Later in this chapter, on pages 34-42, I'll tell you what each of these vitamins and minerals does to help your body function.

Eat Fruit For These Vitamins and Minerals

Apples good source of thiamine and a fair source of calcium, phosphorus, and potassium. Some vitamin A and C, depending on freshness.

Apricots Excellent source of vitamin A and potassium; good source of calcium, phosphorus, and vitamin C.

Bananas Very good source of potassium and vitamin A. Fair source of calcium, phosphorus, and vitamin C.

Blackberries Good amounts of vitamin A and potassium; fair amounts of calcium, phosphorus, and vitamin C.

Blueberries Good iron and magnesium source; fair for vitamins A and C and calcium, phosphorus, and potassium.

Cherries Good source of A, iron, copper, and manganese; fair suppliers of calcium, phosphorus, and potassium. Sour cherries a good source of vitamin C.

Cranberries Small amounts of vitamin C, calcium, phosphorus, and potassium.

Coconut Sodium, potassium, and iron are present in good amounts.

Grapes Good source of vitamin A and potassium, calcium, and phosphorus.

Grapefruit Good source of vitamins C and A; small amounts of potassium, calcium, and phosphorus.

Lemons An excellent source of vitamin C.

Oranges Good to excellent source of vitamins A and C; good source of calcium and folic acid.

Melons Small to excellent amount of vitamin A, depending on the color; good source of vitamin C.

Peaches An excellent source of vitamin A; good source of potassium and niacin and a fair source of vitamin C.

Pears Low in vitamin content but excellent for fiber.

Pineapple Good for vitamin C and potassium.

Plums An excellent source of potassium and a pretty good source of iron and calcium.

Strawberries An excellent source of vitamin C; a good source of vitamin A and calcium, phosphorus, iron, and potassium.

And here are the vegetables, with the feast of nutrients they provide.

Eat Vegetables for These Vitamins and Minerals

Artichokes Good source of vitamins A, B_1, and Riboflavin.

Asparagus Excellent source of vitamins B_1, C, and riboflavin; good source of vitamin A.

Beans (green) Good source of vitamins A, C, and B_1;

Beans (yellow) Excellent source of vitamin B_1; good source of A and C.

Beets Good source of vitamins A, B, and riboflavin; good source of potassium and magnesium.

Broccoli Excellent source of vitamins A, B_1, and C; good source of calcium and potassium.

Brussels Sprouts Excellent source of vitamins A, B_1, and C; good source of calcium and potassium.

Cabbage Good source of vitamins A, B_2, and C; good source of phosphorus, magnesium, and potassium.

Cauliflower   Excellent source of vitamins B_1, C, and riboflavin; good source of phosphorus, magnesium, potassium, and calcium.

Celery   Good source of vitamins A, B_1, and riboflavin and of calcium and phosphorus.

Chard   Excellent source of vitamins A, B_1, C, and riboflavin and of iron.

Chicory   Excellent source of vitamins A, B_1, and C.

Corn   Good source of vitamins A, thiamine, riboflavin, and niacin; also phosphorus, magnesium, iron, and copper.

Cucumbers   Good source of B_1 and riboflavin.

Eggplant   Excellent source of riboflavin; good source of vitamin A.

Endive   Excellent source of riboflavin, calcium, phosphorus, and iron.

Kale   Excellent source of vitamins A, B_1, C, riboflavin, and niacin; good source of all the minerals.

Lettuce   Good source of vitamins A, C, thiamine, and riboflavin.

Mushrooms   Excellent source of potassium, phosphorus, copper, and iron; good source of the B vitamins, thiamine, and riboflavin.

Onions   Good source of potassium; fair source of A, C, calcium, and phosphorus.

Parsnips   Good source of vitamin C and phosphorus, calcium, and potassium.

Peas   Excellent source of vitamin A; good source of vitamin C, thiamine, riboflavin, and niacin as well as of iron, calcium, potassium, and phosphorus.

Peppers   Excellent source of vitamins A and C; good source of calcium, phosphorus, and potassium.

Potatoes   Good source of vitamins C and niacin and of iron, potassium, and phosphorus.

Radishes   Good source of calcium, iron, phosphorus, and potassium.

Spinach   Excellent source of vitamins A, C, and riboflavin; good source of potassium, calcium, and iron.

Scallions   Good source of vitamins A, C, and riboflavin; and of calcium, phosphorus, and potassium.

Squash (summer) Good source of vitamin A and a small amount of C; good source of potassium, phosphorus, and calcium.

Squash (winter) Excellent source of vitamin A; good source of calcium, phosphorus, and potassium.

Sweet potatoes & Yams Excellent source of vitamin A and a good source of C; good source of calcium, potassium, and phosphorus.

Turnips Excellent source of vitamins A and C; good source of calcium, phosphorus, and potassium.

Fruits and vegetables really give you an impressive assortment of nutrients, don't they? You could not possibly go wrong eating any of them, could you? Well, yes. *Sometimes.* It's your body, remember, and you want to look after it as carefully as you can.

What do you have to watch out for with these wonderful, nutrition-packed foods? Once again, it is people, not nature, that keep us on our toes. How are these fruits and vegetables grown and treated before they reach us? Keep these thoughts in mind: Root vegetables—particularly onions, potatoes, and carrots—sometimes are peeled by caustic abrasives, hot steam, even shooting flames; fruit may be peeled by being dipped in a lye (chemical) bath; that shiny surface on your apple, cucumber, green pepper, tomato, or orange may be a paraffin wax dip. In fact, the great color in that tempting-looking piece of fruit may be nothing more than an injected dye.

Food grown in soil that has not been chemically treated—then shipped and stored and stacked and squished—just would not reach you in such beautiful shape! Sometimes you have to make choices. Do you want the colorful, shiny-looking stuff that's been sprayed, injected, or coated, or that less colorful, un-shiny bit of food that has been grown and treated *naturally* all its life? Always you have to ask questions. Ask your local fruit and vegetable stand manager if the food he is selling has been grown or treated with chemicals and insecticides. Try your supermarket's produce department, too, and the nearest health food store. Sometimes a food co-op will be able to help. No one place is guaranteed but you usually can get good answers if you ask good questions. Of course, the best answer—if you and your family can do it—is to grow your own!

If it is winter time now, or if you just want to have some nutritious, delicious fun, try growing sprouts. Sprouts are untreated seeds or dried beans which, when given nourishment (water) will produce tiny stems and leaves—just like the plants in a garden. Sprouts are very rich in vitamins, especially the B-complex, and contain fiber. They really are good in a lot of ways, particularly added to salads and sandwiches.

Carbohydrates on the Run

(**Food Group 2:** Cereals and Baked Goods)

Group 2 covers all grains, breads, and cereal products. What's included? Noodles and other pastas; breads (not just bread, but rolls, muffins, and biscuits, for example, as well); grains like barley, rice, and cracked wheat; breakfast cereals like oatmeal, cream of wheat or rice, and others; even all the baked goods made from white flour (anything made with white flour as the basic ingredient has very little going for it nutritionally). Nutritionists agree that you need four servings from Group 2 daily.

Everyone—*including dieters*—needs the foods in this group. Some people used to believe that eating a lot of bread and grains caused you to gain weight easily. Now we understand that it is the white flour products and the high fat foods that add the unwanted calories. You will especially use this group of foods if you are looking for alternatives to meat and other animal products.

Grains and cereals are important carbohydrate foods. Carbohydrates provide most of the energy you use running around the gym, dancing the Mashed Potato, eating and talking your way through that healthful (I hope!) lunch, even sleeping. Although your muscles are made whole and strong by protein, and your bones are strengthened by calcium, it is the carbohydrates that enable them to function smoothly when you need them. Carbohydrates also provide the energy you need to digest more carbohydrates! As a matter of fact, carbohydrates don't even give up there (Yay, carbohydrates!); they also help digest protein and fat. If we didn't have carbohydrates to burn off for energy, our bodies would be forced to burn off protein. And you need that protein; if you didn't have lots left after the growth and repair of your cells had been taken care of, you would not be in a very healthy state.

Excellent, nourishing foods and just plain junk foods are included in the carbohydrate group. Cakes, pies, candies, and other sweets using sugar, white flour, and fats don't deserve a place in a balanced, nutritious diet. While these so-called "goodies" do offer energy, they do not maintain your energy at a high level or offer any nutrients. (Now I know—and certainly your mom knows—you're going to pack away a little junk food now and then, but *please*...be reasonable!)

Whole grains and flour products, on the other hand, are so important they have been the staple foods of many diets in the world for centuries. Each culture has had its own staple grain, the one they depend on most; rice, for example, in China and Japan.

Besides filling up your belly and giving you energy, grains give us other benefits. Here are some of the ways in which grains, according to many nutritionists, are said to help your body work:

Buckwheat helps the kidneys function smoothly.

Rice may calm and relax your nervous system.

Wheat may aid your liver in carrying out its important job of metabolizing. Barley is reputed to improve digestion.

Wait...that's not all! Grains are also important for the fiber they provide. (If you ever watch television, you must have heard about fiber.) Fiber is also known as roughage. Fiber doesn't include any nutrients or vitamins, but it does help you digest the parts of the food that do. One of the reasons people have more difficulty digesting white flour than whole grains may be the lack of fiber in white flour. The refined carbohydrates in white flour are broken down so quickly they cause a sharp rise, then a sudden fall, in your blood sugar. You may have heard the low blood sugar condition called hypoglycemia.

Do you sometimes feel tired, anxious, or irritable—maybe a little bit cranky and you don't even know why—after eating a starchy and refined food? You can get the same kind of reaction from eating candy and other sugary foods, too. While whole grains turn into a sugar called maltose when they are digested, candy and other sweets convert into a different kind of sugar called sucrose. Sucrose is another name for the common white sugar in your sugar bowl at home. Regardless of which form sugar takes, your body uses it as a carbohydrate; however, it handles different forms of sugar in different ways.

Both sucrose and maltose are formed by two sugars stuck together. White sugar, however, is so concentrated and refined that it has no nutrients or fiber for our bodies to digest. As a result, any white sugar we eat zips into our bloodstream, gives us a quick jolt of energy, and zips right out again— leaving us hungrier, and less energetic, than we were before. You can eat pounds of white sugar (sucrose) every day and still feel hungry, because without the nutrients your poor body doesn't even know it's been fed!

Maltose, on the other hand, is more slowly digested. It has to follow the usual path of digestion, through your intestinal tract, over to your liver, and into your cells, to rest until you need energy. "Good" carbohydrates store so well, and are released so quickly when you need them, that they are now considered the very best source of energy—even ahead of that old favorite, protein.

How do you know if you are not getting enough carbohydrates? Since most of the vitamins and minerals you need are included in grains, beans, seeds, vegetables, and fruits, it's hard to end up with a deficiency. If you do, it probably will be the result of eating too much junk food or too much protein. If you are deficient in carbohydrates, you certainly will feel it! Reliable clues that tell you you probably have that condition include a droopy, rundown feeling (having less energy and stamina than you usually do); getting sick more often (catching a cold or the flu much more than your family and friends do); and feeling grumpy and irritable. Check the chart on vitamins and minerals (pages 34–42) for more information on specific problems and ways to correct them.

Calcium: NOT Just From Milk

(Food Group 3: Milk and Milk Products)

The milk and milk products in this group meet our bodies' needs for calcium and phosphorus. While all of the minerals are needed by our bodies for good health, calcium is needed in the largest amounts. Ninety-nine per cent (99%) of the calcium we take in through eating is stored in our bones and teeth. This calcium provides a network of thin lines which weave together and hold all the nutrients and other materials together. But it isn't just your bones and teeth that need calcium. Your entire body depends on it for the muscle strength it gives you. Your heart, your most important and life-giving muscle, can't contract and relax (in other words, beat) without calcium. Neither can blood clot properly without it. If you cut yourself, you would just keep on bleeding—without the help of calcium.

That one per cent (1%) of the calcium that isn't stored is equally necessary, in its own way. Without that little bit of calcium that doesn't go to your bones and teeth, your nerve impulses wouldn't function. All the enzymes needed to get your body processes moving would be at a standstill without calcium to spur them on. Calcium helps you make use of other vitamins and minerals you get in food, too. Vitamin B_{12} is more easily absorbed if it is eaten in combination with calcium-containing foods. Protein is also. Calcium itself benefits from food-combining. Eating protein-rich foods, getting sufficient vitamin D (the "sunshine vitamin"), and always taking in enough phosphorus can help you absorb calcium well.

Certain foods high in calcium, such as spinach, chard, rhubarb, and beet greens (the tops) have in them something called oxalic acid. Oxalic acid, a chemical with two parts, combines with calcium-rich foods *to prevent* calcium from being used by your body. Cocoa and chocolate form this chemical when mixed with milk. This fact worries many people who rely on plant foods for their calcium intake. Other people wonder how most of the world has stayed healthy for thousands of years without using dairy products in their diets. Now we know that much of the oxalic acid can be drained off in the water used to cook leafy green vegetables mentioned earlier in this paragraph, or the vegetables can be eaten raw. Still, it is not a smart idea to depend on those foods to give you the calcium you need.

Fluoride, the chemical that is put in many water supplies, and which is found naturally in such foods as seafood and tea, can also bind calcium and make it unavailable to your body. Too much of a good thing, protein, is another "calcium fighter" to watch out for. The more protein you eat, the more calcium you need to balance it. People who eat a diet that's high in both calcium and protein may always find themselves deficient in protein, no matter how much they consume! Foods that are high in both nutrients are cheeses, milk products other than milk, and eggs.

Remember your parents telling you that exercise would help make you healthy and strong? Turns out they were right again. Invalids and other hospitalized or bedridden people lose much of the calcium from their bones. Running, jumping, dancing, and all other forms of exercise help your bones retain calcium. And while you're outside running around, vitamin D is being metabolized in your body by the sunlight, helping you metabolize calcium at the same time.

This food group usually has meant milk and milk products to the people in our country, and those foods are indeed an excellent source of calcium and phosphorus. Phosphorus is needed by our bodies in equal, or slightly more than equal, amounts as calcium. Conveniently, the foods which supply us with calcium usually furnish an equal amount of phosphorus. Pretty much the same bodily functions are aided by phosphorus, too. You really don't have to worry, then, unless you eat too much meat or drink too many sodas—both of which contain high levels of phosphorus. *Too much* phosphorus would put us in the same condition we would be in if we had *too little* calcium.

Probably the best known example of a calcium deficiency is rickets. This condition, a bone problem many kids have heard or read about, is the most extreme example of poor bone formation caused by too little calcium. There are other serious, but less critical, signs of the same problem. Older adults sometimes develop painful conditions, in which either their bones become softer and change form or just the opposite happens; their bones become brittle and break more easily. Although you won't suffer those effects while you are young, nutritionists suggest it is partially your calcium intake as a teenager that determines the condition of your bones when you are older.

There are other indications of too little calcium in your diet that are not as serious but can make daily living a little less wonderful. It's hard to be happy with a calcium deficiency! *Grumpy, negative,* and *impossible to please* would be good definitions of your behavior if you were calcium deficient. A person lacking calcium is, on the one hand, too tired to really do much; on the other hand, too restless and fidgety to sit still!

Does that sound like anyone you know? Come on, beside your kid brother! An interesting clue to a calcium problem is how much milk, cheese, and ice cream you eat. A person who is lacking calcium seems to crave the foods that contain it. By itself, that isn't so interesting; if your body needs something, it's pretty wise to crave it, to want to have as much as possible. The interesting, and unfortunate, aspect of this particular problem is that many of the people who crave dairy products because their bodies need the calcium don't get any benefit from the dairy products they eat. Their systems cannot absorb the calcium in the dairy products! What do these people do?

Folks in this country love those dairy foods! Some, though, can't, won't, or don't want to eat them. There are various reasons for this. Although we are accustomed to hearing how healthful milk products are (from groups like the American Dairy Association), new research findings tell us this may not be so. One reason for these different points of view is the high fat content of most milk products. This fat seems to settle around the vital organs of some people. The organs most affected are the kidney, the gall bladder, and the reproductive organs. Whole milk, cream, cream cheese, and salty, hard cheeses seem to be the major high fat content contributors.

Skin problems, like eczema and acne, worsen for some kids after the consumption of too much butter. Congestion in your nose, chest, and lungs can be another unpleasant side effect. Many girls and women find their menstrual cramps are relieved when they cut down on dairy products. It seems even your brain can be affected. Is it just coincidence that your brain may become sluggish and slow just after you have finished that milkshake? Many people think not.

Perhaps this explains why it was less than two hundred years ago that humankind considered using a cow's milk for their own consumption and pleasure instead of just saving it for the baby calf. Our ancestors before that time may have had more instinctive wisdom about their bodies than we seem to now. Maybe farmers who turned to human use of cows' milk for the first time had lost their crops to drought or insects, and had developed strong cravings for calcium. Of course, they would not have known then that it was calcium that they wanted or needed. Like so many other discoveries in history, they might have drunk some of their cows' milk by accident, or because there was little other food available, and found their cravings satisfied. Who knows?

Let's get back to the people who crave dairy products but whose bodies cannot absorb the calcium in them. A growing number of kids and adults are being told, or learning by themselves, that they have an allergy to milk. A person who is allergic to milk won't be able to use any of the nutrients he or she will be swallowing! Kids who were unable to drink milk as babies often turn out to be allergic as they grow older. Do you get colds more often than most of your friends do? Could be an allergy. Do you have any of these symptoms of an allergic reaction to milk?

hay fever
headaches
hives
asthma
tiredness
diarrhea
bloated stomach
heavy sweating
dizziness
low blood sugar
hyperactivity

If you feel you may be allergic to milk and milk products, or maybe to other foods, talk to your parents and to your doctor. You may have an allergic condition that not only affects how you feel physically, it can also bother you emotionally and maybe even affect your ability to do your best in school. Or you may have a condition called lactose intolerance. This condition, becoming more common all the time, can imitate the symptoms of a milk allergy. When you are lactose intolerant, unable to tolerate milk, you are actually reacting to *lactose*—the sugar in milk. Some people don't have an enzyme, called *lactase*, in their bodies in a sufficient amount to digest lactose, the milk sugar. This is a common condition for most of the world's population and a problem for many Americans. Black Americans, American Indians, and Americans with Asian, Eastern-European, and Southern-European ancestors are especially apt to be lactose intolerant.

Some individuals have enough of the lactase enzyme in their systems when they are children but lose it when they grow older. Some other people have a limited amount of lactase; while they can't digest milk, butter, and some cheeses they can eat yogurt and other fermented milk products. If you have diarrhea, a bloated stomach, or cramps after drinking or eating milk products, you may want to have a simple blood test to see if you have this problem. If you find you do, you may want to read one of the few good books written on this subject, *Living...Without Milk*, by Jacqueline Hostage (also published by Betterway Publications).

Too much milk may not cause any of the troublesome conditions I have listed (or another troublesome condition that could be particularly embarrassing in school), *but* it may just destroy the very vitamins you expect it to add to your diet—vitamin D and phosphorus.

Researchers also have learned that, in reasonable amounts, calcium can screen out harmful environmental pollutants and radiation, as well as improve digestion. To much, though, and the digestive process is aggravated. The more we learn, the more we appreciate the wisdom of the saying "Moderation in all things." (Hasn't your mother said that to you? Mine did, again and again. Guess I needed it!)

If you are concerned about milk and milk products in your diet—maybe you think you have some of the symptoms of milk allergy or lactose intolerance I pointed out earlier—and you are confused about where else except from dairy products you can get all-important supplies of calcium and phosphorus, keep reading. But remember, don't make any important decisions about your diet by yourself. Talk to your parents first; if they agree, then talk to your doctor.

There are many rich calcium alternatives in the plant foods families. While we mentioned possible problems with certain leafy green vegetables that contain oxalic acid and therefore were not very useful sources of calcium, there are other greens that are very good. Turnip greens, collards, kale, mustard greens, broccoli, and green beans are all excellent sources. It's a shame that most people have gotten away from eating a variety of greens; because of that, it is often hard to find some of those I listed in the super-market. Fortunately, there are other good calcium sources; bean sprouts, for example, which you can grow anytime, are very good. Nuts, especially al-monds, are tasty calcium suppliers. (Carry a little bag of almonds to munch on when you're worrying about that big exam!) Soybeans are an excep-tionally rich calcium source, but you could have a problem with too much protein if you ate too much of that versatile food. (More about soybeans later.)

Other dried beans are good also. Brazil nuts, not used very commonly for some reason, are an even better calcium source than almonds; a cup of Brazil nuts has about the same amount of calcium as a cup of cow's milk. Sesame seeds are wonderful when it comes to calcium, and excellent for phosphorus, too. Make up a pitcher of sesame "milk" (see page 55) and use it to replace cow's milk. At ten times the calcium content of cow's milk, sesame "milk" gives you a nutritional bonanza.

Most foods have some calcium and phosphorus in them. Whole grains, potatoes, fresh fruits, and honey are fair sources. Eggs and fish are pretty good, too. Phosphorus is particularly plentiful in wheat germ and rice bran, as well as in high calcium content foods. A magnificent source that you probably have not heard of is sea vegetables, otherwise known as...are you ready for this?...seaweed! Asian people around the world, as well as resi-dents of coastal towns in Canada, Maine, Hawaii, and elsewhere have known about, and eaten, this nutrition-packed food for ages. Kelp, which is widely used, dried and flaked or powdered, as a substitute for salt, gives you the cal-cium equivalent of Cheddar cheese—the highest dairy product source of cal-cium. Dulse, another easily-digested variety, has as much calcium as Brazil nuts; and agar, a variety commonly used as a thickener and a gelatin-type treat, has twice that of sesame seeds. More about sea vegetables later.

If you do use plant foods, rather than dairy products, for your calcium in-take, you have to compensate for the lack of vitamin D in plant foods. The only really great source of vitamin D, outside of dairy products, is sunflower seeds. Other good animal sources, outside of dairy products, are fatty fish (like tuna and salmon) and oysters. Not to worry, however. As you know, you body can synthesize (make) vitamin D from natural sunshine. While you are exercising out in the sun, you should get plenty!

Plentiful Protein

(Food Group 4: Meat and Meat Alternatives)

Group 4 is the meat group—actually meat, fowl, fish, and beans—and our #1 supplier of protein. Protein is our most necessary nutrient. In fact, it is the foundation of the more than one hundred trillion cells in our body. Like the other nutrients, protein contains the elements oxygen, hydrogen, and carbon. Unlike the others, it also contains nitrogen. It is the addition of nitrogen that enables our bodies to grow, our cells to regenerate themselves. Without protein we would not be able to build the new cells needed to make our tissues. As much as three to five per cent of the protein in your body is replaced each day. Just do a little simple arithmetic and you'll see that you are not really the kid you were even a few weeks ago! Our bodies wouldn't be able to produce hemoglobin either; that's the substance in our blood that carries oxygen from our lungs to our tissues and it is ninety-five per cent (95%) protein. Protein is used in the formation of antibodies, which help protect us from illness.

One of protein's most unusual characteristics is its ability to change, depending on what each group of cells may need at the moment. For example, it is the protein that goes to our muscles that turns a watery substance into a firm and springy one. You may have wondered why sick, bedridden people of all ages often look slack, maybe even a little bit shrunken. When a person is suffering from the stress of illness, his or her body puts the available protein to work healing, not building up muscle tone and strength.

Protein forms a protective coating on your hair and nails, giving them a healthy shine (if you are getting enough protein in your diet). People lacking in protein often have dull, dry, cracked hair and nails because of this.

Protein is especially important to you as you as you are growing up, before you reach the age of twenty. Until that time, you are considered to be in a *positive balance*, because you are taking in more protein than you are letting out. Between ten and twelve, as you enter adolescence, you experience a major growth spurt. At this age, you probably are getting more actively and energetically involved in sports. If you want to play up to the best of your ability, you will need to maintain an adequate protein intake. Athletes depend on a good supply of protein for muscle strength and stamina.

Girls, when they begin menstruating, will want to maintain a steady protein intake so their potassium-sodium balance isn't disrupted. If this balance is not maintained, a girl could experience edema (water retention), one of the causes of menstrual cramps and water weight gain.

Going through adolescence and the few years following means a lot of stress to every young person, physical stress and mental stress. All the hormone changes your body goes through during adolescence depend on protein to happen smoothly.

Since you use so much protein every day to maintain your health and to grow, you need to be certain you are supplying your body with all that it needs. One way of doing this would be to eat some of the foods included in Group 4. For example, one softboiled egg for breakfast, a cheese sandwich for lunch, and a quarter-pound hamburger for dinner (at home, not at a well-known hamburger stand!) would give about 52 grams of protein. The current recommended daily intake of protein for kids ten to fourteen is 46 grams.

There are other ways of getting enough protein besides eating animal products—meat, fish, eggs, etc. You probably know people who are vegetarians, who eat no meat at all. For many different reasons, people are questioning our country's enormous diet dependency on animal foods.

More than two-thirds of the world's diet consists of cereal grains. While it is true that many, many people in the world are undernourished, suffering from malnutrition, even starving from a lack of protein in their diets, it is equally true that we in this country are at best overfed and at worst unhealthy, from too much protein and other rich foods.

America has been blessed with a wonderful environment for farming. For a number of reasons, we have chosen to use much of our land to raise beef cattle and other livestock. About half of the grain and beans planted on our farms is used to feed these animals. The animals, in turn, are slaughtered to feed people. For every pound of roast beef on your table at dinner, a cow has eaten twenty-one pounds of grain. Since plants are the original source of protein—they make it from the soil, air, sunlight, and water—eating protein in the form of meat is called *eating at the top of the food chain.*

Many people recommend getting off the *top* and eating further down the food chain by eating the grains normally fed to cattle and other animals. These grains are usually corn, barley, oats, soybeans, wheat, and rye. If you were to eat grains rather than meat, you could save five acres of farmland that would have gone toward raising livestock. Eating soybeans, dried beans, and peas would save ten acres. And if you were to eat leafy green vegetables instead of having them fed to animals, you could save fifteen acres.

We have so much in this country that it is hard to imagine that many— millions and millions—of our neighbors in this world are starving. Not only do a lot of people believe we have the responsibility to use our greatest national wealth, the output of our farms, more wisely, the research of many food experts—nutritionists and other scientists—indicates we will feel better if we eat less meat. An apparent side effect of *eating at the top of the food chain* is the generally worsening state of our nation's health.

In order to harvest a plumper cattle crop more quickly, and to prevent disease from spreading in crowded pens and pastures, the animals often are fed with grain laced with antibiotics or hormones. Some people are allergic to these substances and find themselves sick after eating meat. Other people, while not allergic, develop a build-up of antibiotics in their bodies' tissues. Then, when they become sick and their doctors prescribe antibiotics to "cure" them, they find these drugs no longer work for them.

You may find yourself sleepy and tired after eating meat, because of the tranquilizers injected into the cows' muscles to make them more tender. Animals have such a high fat content that the antibiotics—or anything else—

stays trapped in their fat. We humans have the same problem with our fat. When we, in turn, eat that hamburger or steak, we eat that high fat content. This fat problem bothers health conscious people for other reasons also, since the "health troubles ahead" signs seem to be increasing along with our consumption of animal foods.

Some of the health disorders linked to a high dietary fat content include certain types of cancer (especially in fatty glands like the breast or the reproductive organs), heart disease, high cholesterol—leading to arterial diseases, and obesity.

Time for a commercial, and a reminder of the "all things in moderation" theme. If you treat animal foods as one element in a balanced diet—a little beef, a few eggs, some seafood, lots of green vegetables, some grains, beans, fruit, and so forth—you and your body should "go together" for a long, long time.

Speaking of moderation, too much of almost anything can be a bad thing. If you have too much protein, your kidneys may become enlarged because they are overworked trying to push through all that protein. Your bones may begin to lose calcium because the delicate balance between calcium and phosphorus has been lost. And the liver may become enlarged also, from trying to break down all those amino acids.

What are amino acids? Amino acids are what you have when the protein in food is broken down by digestion. I want to tell you more about this important subject, and more about what you need to know to plan a healthy diet using alternatives to meat and other animal products.

Amino acids usually are called the "building blocks" of protein. That is because there are twenty-two of these little molecules, the smallest parts of your cells, needed to make one big protein molecule.

Our bodies can produce all but eight of these amino acids without our awareness or assistance. The remaining eight are called the **essential amino acids.** This doesn't mean that the other fourteen are less important. It does mean that it is important and essential to our existence that we get the essential eight from our daily diets. When a food contains all eight of these essential amino acids it is called a *complete protein.* Complete protein comes almost completely from animal sources. All meats and poultry, fish and seafood, eggs and cheeses are complete proteins. Some vegetable foods, like sunflower and sesame seeds, wheat germ, and nuts are almost complete. One vegetable, the soybean, is complete.

Complete protein foods are capable of sustaining life; in other words, keeping you alive and healthy. Foods that cannot sustain life but that contain *some* of the essential eight amino acids are called *incomplete proteins.* Incomplete proteins can be put together in certain combinations to make complete proteins. Some foods which contain incomplete protein include:

all cereal grains
all nuts
legumes
dry peas
peanuts
avocados
olives
coconuts
all seeds

There are many, many ways to combine these plant foods in a tasty way to come up with as much protein as meat and meat products provide. Here are some of the ways you could mix and match the above foods:

corn and beans
rice and beans
wheat and beans
nuts and beans
seeds and beans

If you also use milk and milk products in your diet, you can add these combinations:

milk and beans
milk and wheat
milk and potato

Even more combinations can be made by using three foods instead of two. There are a lot of examples of people all over the world eating this way: Latin Americans who eat corn tortillas with black beans; Indians who rely on wheat chapatis and chick peas; Arabs who consume a lot of rice and soy. Try to find out what your ancestors ate. You might get a clue to the types of food that will appeal to your taste buds and contribute to your good health.

There is one very important point to remember about eating this way; that is, about combining incomplete protein foods in ways that give you the complete protein you need. All complementary foods should be eaten at the same meal—or, at least, within a short time of each other. Since your food is digested within about four hours, lunch can't possibly complement, and mix with, dinner to give you the nutritional benefits of combining.

Another fact to consider when combining incomplete protein foods is how well your body can digest the combination. The "bunches" of amino acids that make up protein differ depending on their types. There may be three or three thousand amino acids in one bunch. All foods are judged in comparison with the egg, which has a "protein efficiency rate" of 94%. This means that 94% of the protein in an egg can be used by your body.

Here is a chart to help you combine foods for complete protein:

COMBINING FOODS FOR COMPLETE PROTEIN

Combine this food:	With this food:
Milk products: (including milk, cheese, yogurt, etc.)	Rice Potatoes Corn *and* soy products Beans Wheat Peanuts Sesame seeds Wheat *and* peanuts
Dried beans and legumes: (including black-eyed peas, chick-peas, kidney, lima, navy or pinto beans, and lentils)	Milk products Corn Rice Wheat Sesame seeds
Soybeans† or soy products: (including tofu, tamari, miso, etc.)	Corn Sesame seeds *and* wheat Rice *and* wheat Corn *and* milk products Peanuts *and* sesame seeds
Peanuts†:	Milk Wheat *and* soy products Sunflower seeds Wheat *and* milk products
Sesame seeds:	Beans or legumes Rice Soy products *and* wheat
Corn:	Beans or legumes
Rice:	Beans or legumes Sesame seeds Milk products
Wheat:	Beans or legumes Milk products Milk products *and* peanuts Soy products *and* sesame seeds

†Peanuts and soybeans are actually legumes.

Meats and other animal foods supply us with more usable protein than plant foods. That means you must eat more plant foods to get the same amount of protein you would get from smaller portions of meat and other animal products.

Some foods are particularly helpful because they give the most protein for the number of calories they provide (especially important to calorie counters). Fish, chicken, and soybeans lead this list, with lentils, mungbeans, chick-peas, and sunflower seeds following closely behind. Meat and dairy products are disqualified in this comparison because of their high fat contents. (Fat has the most calories.) The grains with the most protein to offer are wheat, rye and oats. If you are interested in welcoming more plant foods into your life, it would be a good idea to make a copy of the **Combining Foods for Complete Protein** chart. Tape it to the side of the refrigerator or onto a cabinet door. Then it's easy to check the chart, and maybe throw a handful of seeds or nuts on your supper or cereal.

Remember, if you are missing *even one* of those eight essential amino acids, the protein level of the seven you do eat will fall back to the level of the low-est one, and you will have lost almost all of the benefits you might have had from combining.

We Americans get more protein than we need from our diets—70% more than much of the rest of the world—but that does not change the fact that each of us needs the right amount, the protein we need to build and repair our bodies. That amount may be different for you than it is for your brother and friend. Stay in touch with how your body feels and looks. A protein deficiency may reveal itself in a number of ways. Check the condition of your hair, skin, and nails. Are they strong and vibrant looking? How about your muscle tone? A flabby muscle or two could just be the result of not enough exercise, but a general muscle weakness could reflect a lack of protein.

Protein affects your ability to resist illness and infection, and determines how quickly you bounce back after you have been sick. In all areas, you will notice a greater ability to handle both physical and mental stress, if you have the needed amount of protein.

If you are very energetic you may be able to burn off any extra protein as energy. If you enjoy reading or more quiet activities, you probably would keep any extra protein in the form of fat. Later in this section, we'll get to some of the really super protein suppliers, like soybeans, in more detail.

It's time, I think, for a little summing up. If you have been paying atten-tion (if you have, you know by now that the more intelligently you eat, the better you can—pay attention, that is), you have learned quite a bit about nutrition, about the *four basic food groups*, about *nutritious alternatives to meat and dairy products*, and about *protein* and *protein food combinations*. Now, let's get into digestion.

From Here to Digestion

If you want to be a vital, growing human being, you need to take in foods from the four food groups you have just read about. And then you need to digest them. After your nose directs your attention to those tempting smells rising from the plate in front of you, and before you swallow, give your teeth a chance do do their thing. Maybe they are in braces now, but put 'em to work. Your stomach will thank you if you spend a silent moment chewing each bite before it slides down your throat.

You have thirty-two teeth; eight to chomp on those vegetables and fruits, four for tearing into flesh foods, and twenty for grinding cereal grains. (Maybe we should consider that breakdown a reasonable distribution of the foods we should eat.)

Your mouth contains an enzyme called ptylin that breaks down carbo-hydrates. The better you chew your food, the more saliva you will produce and the less work you pass on to the rest of your digestive system. Not only does this make you feel better, it leaves you the energy for something more interesting than digesting your food!

After you swallow, the chewed food goes down the esophagus, while gentle waves are produced by an action called peristalsis. In the center of your stomach, the food is combined with gastric juices. How you felt when you were eating has a lot to do with the condition of your gastric juices. If you were worried, angry, sad, or sick, your gastric juices will not have created a very healthy environment for the food that was on the way. In one to four hours, the food—which is now in a liquid state called chyme—is forced out of the stomach and into the small intestine. Your small intestine is crucial to your health because it absorbs the vitamins and minerals from your food. Now the pancreas gets into the act. Different types of enzymes are produced by the pancreas, depending on what you have eaten. Any food that is still undigested now goes into the large intestine, where it stays until it is carried out of your body as waste.

By now, the digested food has been turned into glucose, amino acids, fatty acids, and glycerol, and is passing into your bloodstream (by osmosis) to carry on the work of your life.

Vitamins, vitamins, and Minerals, Too

It's a good feeling to learn more about your body, isn't it? To understand that you can really influence the way you look, act, and feel—even think— by the way you feed and nourish yourself. To begin making some decisions that will influence how you and your body will get along for the rest of your life. After all, it is your body—your *only* body. Make the most of it!

Old-fashioned sayings ("Make the most of it" is a good example!) get to be a little boring sometimes, but they stick around and people—parents and teachers especially—still use them because they make sense. Maybe they're a little dull, but they are true. "All things in moderation." "You are what you eat." I know...boring, boring, boring...but still true. And how about this: "I'm telling you this for your own good." If you are ten or eleven now, maybe you have heard this only about 250 times. If you are thirteen or fourteen, you probably have lost count...so maybe hearing it one more time won't hurt. Please read the following pages carefully; it's the last hard-working sec- tion before the fun of making a lot of the good recipes that follow. Pay atten- tion...**It's for your own good!**

When you learn about vitamins and minerals, you will be in a better position to judge what you need to stay healthy. All whole foods contain nutrients; that is, vitamins and minerals. Since we are all individuals, we all have different needs. For most people a balanced diet will be enough all by itself. Sometimes, however, you may find you have an unusual amount of stress in your life. It could be from problems in school. Or maybe you have moved and you need to make all new friends; sometimes that's hard. Or maybe an allergy or two is upsetting you physically or emotionally. Any of these stress conditions will put extra demands on your body. You'll need more of certain vitamins and minerals than you would if just about every- thing in your life was normal and pretty relaxed.

Read the chart coming up on vitamins and minerals (coming up on pages 34–42). If you feel a cold coming on, "doctor yourself" with a double portion of broccoli. Feed that after-school frazzle with a handful of sunflower seeds.

Most authorities recommend getting your vitamins and minerals from food rather than pills and injections. If in some cases it seems as though maybe you should take vitamins as well, it's better and safer to see a doctor before making your own diagnosis. A few vitamins store themselves in your fat and can become toxic (poisonous) if taken in excess. In any case, like amino acids, if even one is missing it throws the whole process out of whack and none of the vitamins you "eat" get properly utilized. With whole, un- processed foods new to many of our diets, we probably are getting traces of minerals we need that science hasn't even discovered yet; like vitamin B_{12}, for example, which was found only thirty years ago. It is probably safe to say that we have not yet unlocked all the secrets of nature.

VITAMINS AND MINERALS

VITAMIN A is a fat soluble vitamin which helps repair our body tissues and protects the inside of our mouths, noses, throats and lungs from foreign germs and dirt. It also fights air and environmental pollutants. It aids us in digesting protein and building the health of our blood, bones, teeth, and eyes.

Where can you find it? Carrots, beet greens, broccoli, and spinach are your best bets.

What happens if you don't get enough? Night blindness and dry or blemished skin are common signs. You may feel tired and have a loss of appetite, too.

What happens if you get too much? The fact that vitamin A is a fat soluble vitamin means too much could be stored in your body fat. Some people who eat a lot of animal products get too much vitamin A because animals store it in their fat. Some of the signs you may be getting too much are nausea, headaches, and diarrhea.

B COMPLEX VITAMINS are water soluble vitamins grown or developed from mold.

VITAMIN B_1, or THIAMINE, as it is also called, helps us to digest carbohydrates. Healthy nerves, muscle tone, and our ability to learn are all aided by adequate supplies of vitamin B_1.

Where can you find it? Wheat and wheat germ, brown rice, and other whole grains, and brewers yeast are the best sources.

What happens if you don't get enough? Eating sugary foods and smoking cigarettes use up lots of this vitamin, as does being under stress. Having difficulty breathing, feeling tired, feeling grumpy and emotionally out of sorts, and forgetting things are some possible signs of a B_1 deficiency.

What happens if you get too much? Nothing. Since it is a water soluble vitamin, that means that any extra your body cannot use is eliminated in your urine.

VITAMIN B_2, also known as **RIBOFLAVIN,** also helps us digest carbohydrates. Like all the other B vitamins, the enzymes needed for all of our bodies' functions are produced here. B_2 also helps the digestion of fats and protein. Our eyesight, skin, nails, and hair get a boost and our emotions are more relaxed and calm.

Where can you find it? Liver and brewers yeast are the richest sources, but all whole grains and unprocessed foods contain some B_2.

What happens if you don't get enough? One of the first signals is cracks in the corners of your mouth. Sometimes your eyes will feel hot and gritty. A sensitivity to light is also common. However, unless you really eat a lot of junk or have some problem utilizing the food you eat, it's unlikely you will have a vitamin B_2 deficiency.

What happens if you get too much? Again, nothing at all—with the possible exception of having to go to the bathroom more often to get rid of all those extra vitamins!

VITAMIN B₆, or PYRIDOXINE, is needed to absorb vitamin B_{12}, and helps in the production of hydrocholine acid and in the digestion of carbohydrates, fats, and proteins. Red blood cells need B_6 to prevent a type of anemia, and your sodium-potassium balance depends on this vitamin to produce the glycogen needed for energy.

Where can you find it? Meat, whole grains, and brewers yeast are the best sources. Peanuts and most vegetables contain less, but because they are usually cooked for a shorter time they retain more. Well-cooked meat contains very little of it.

What happens if you don't get enough? Vitamin B_6 is needed to enable many of our enzymes to work at all. If you have a deficiency, the problems can be quite varied. Hypoglycemia, or low blood sugar, is becoming more common as our foods become more processed and vitamin B_6 is milled from our grains. If your hair starts falling out, your arms and legs (or hands and feet) feel numb and weak, and you are retaining water you may have a lack of B_6 in your diet. A deficiency in B_6 also can cause cracks in your mouth and affect your ability to learn—and to understand what you are learning.

What happens if you get too much? At this point in your life, nothing.

VITAMIN B₁₂ also works with other B vitamins to help you digest protein, fats, and carbohydrates. It helps you maintain a calm disposition as well as boosting your utilization of iron, which also helps your nervous system. Vitamin B_{12} has a very important job in helping your body synthesize fatty acids, too. Without fatty acids, you wouldn't have much energy.

Where can you find it? Meats, fish, eggs, and dairy products are the main sources of B_{12}. The only known vegetable sources are fermented soy products, such as tempeh and miso.

What happens if you don't get enough? This has been one of the few worries of total vegetarians—people who don't eat any animal products, including dairy products and eggs. Some new research suggests that people who eat a diet based on whole foods need less B_{12} than those who eat mostly refined and processed foods. Why? Most commercial food has a preservative called propionate that is put in to kill any bacteria or mold that might develop. However, eliminating the bacteria and mold also destroys the B_{12}. When this propionate gets into your bloodstream it's thought also to kill off the B_{12} already there. It's odd, I know, but eating too many dairy products and meat can increase your need for vitamin B_{12}. So, what happens if you don't get enough B_{12}; that is, if your body does not utilize enough? Your nervous system is affected. Your reflexes may suffer, you may develop a "pins and needles" feeling in your hands and feet, and you are apt to have a nervous and anxious outlook on life. Girls and women can experience menstrual difficulties and hot and cold flashes. These are less threat-threatening effects of too little B_{12}. The most dangerous possible effect of too little B_{12} is pernicious anemia, a condition that develops in cases of extreme deficiency only.

What happens if you get too much? Unlikely to be a problem.

BIOTIN, another of the B vitamins, is also an important factor in stabilizing your fatty acids. Biotin also helps you utilize protein, folic acid, pantothenic acid, and vitamin B_{12}. Its real starring role is keeping the carbon dioxide moving in your blood.

Where can we find it? Biotin is another one of those nutrients we'll get plenty of if we eat whole foods. The best sources are brown rice, egg yolk, liver, and brewer's yeast.

What happens if you don't get enough? This does not seem to be much of a problem. Because saccharin binds biotin in your body, you should try to avoid it (easy on the diet sodas!). Raw egg whites also could interfere with your body's ability to utilize biotin, but you are unlikely to have raw egg whites very often.

What happens if you get too much? Just as it is very unlikely you will be deficient, it's just as unlikely you will have too much.

CHOLINE, another B vitamin, is a component in lecithin, and helps you use and break down fats and cholesterol. Choline greatly promotes the health of your liver and kidneys.

Where can we find it? The best sources are, once again, egg yolk, liver, brewers yeast, and all whole grains. Wheat is especially good, as are rice, soybeans, chick peas, lentils, and split green peas.

What happens if you don't get enough? Not likely, if you eat a balanced diet.

What happens if you get too much? Your own inner family of bacteria think choline makes such an enjoyable snack that you never have too much in your system.

FOLIC ACID is a B vitamin with a simple mission. Helping you build healthy blood is just about all this vitamin contributes. However, it also helps your body form nucleic acid and contributes to the well-being of your liver.

Where can we find it? Here's a chance for those leafy, green vegetables to shine. They are the leading contributors, along with liver and brewers yeast. Whole grains, especially wheat and rice, and dried beans and peas (soybeans in particular) are almost as good.

What happens if you don't get enough? This seems to be fairly common in our country. Women, in particular, have a tendency to be deficient. In fact, fifty per cent (50%) are said to be lacking in folic acid. In other words, they are anemic. Other signs of a deficiency are a growth slowdown (in kids), intestinal and digestive problems, and some forms of mental illness.

What happens if you get too much? Most of us do not have to worry, since there is little chance we eat too much liver or too many green vegetables. There is concern that too much folic acid can contribute to serious health problems. Because of that, it is now against the law to get high potency folic acid without a doctor's prescription.

NIACIN is the B vitamin most responsible for keeping your circulation moving. Like the others, it is also instrumental in helping to break down protein, carbohydrates, and fats, reducing the cholesterol level in your blood. Niacin helps keep your skin clear and your nervous system calm and relaxed.

Where can we find it? Niacin is most prevalent in meat, poultry, fish, peanuts, wheat germ, and brewers yeast. Sesame and sunflower seeds, nuts, and wholegrains also are good sources.

What happens if you don't get enough? If you maintain a good, balanced diet, you will not have any problems with niacin. Deficiencies are caused primarily by too much consumption of sugar and white flour. If you are taking antibiotics, which are destructive of niacin, you could have a temporary problem. The most common indications of a niacin deficiency are cankers and cold sores.

What happens if you get too much? Niacin is one of the vitamins most often used in mega-vitamin therapy. Too much of this vitamin can aggravate ulcers or cause damage to your liver, so don't decide to be your own doctor, prescribing too many vitamins for yourself.

VITAMIN C is another water soluble vitamin, probably the most famous one. Vitamin C is so important for several reasons. First, it maintains the connective tissue that runs between our skin and bones. Second, it helps to grow scar tissue. And by helping to form red blood cells it aids us in resisting infections and allergies.

Where can we find it? Green peppers, strawberries, spinach and other leafy greens, citrus fruits, cabbage, and scallions all are very good sources. Lots of other foods contain lesser amounts as well.

What happens if you don't get enough? It's pretty easy to find yourself with too little vitamin C. Stress, fever and illness—and antibiotics, aspirin, cigarettes, baking soda, and pollution are some of the major vitamin C destroyers. Some of the signs that you are being deprived are shortness of breath, anemia, poor healing, getting sick more easily, and having indigestion often. Some foods that many people believe saturate them with vitamin C, such as frozen orange juice and cooked green vegetables, are nearly worthless unless you mix and cook with pure water. Tap water will add copper to your juice or vegetables, and copper destroys the good effects of vitamin C. Eating green vegetables is good *if* you cook them in just a little water over fairly low heat.

Otherwise, the heat will kill the vitamins. Lots of us try to take large amounts of vitamin C, in both food and pill form, when we feel a cold coming on. This tends to be effective if you begin the "treatment" when the first cold symptoms appear.

What happens if you get too much? So far the only known problems associated with mega-doses of vitamin C are diarrhea and increased frequency of urination. There are no known problems from eating too many foods rich in vitamin C.

VITAMIN D is also a fat soluble vitamin, known as the "Sunshine Vitamin." This is because the sun activates a form of cholesterol in our skin and turns it into vitamin D. We need this vitamin for its help in absorbing calcium and the breakdown of phosphorus. Children must have it to help form their bones and teeth. For all of us, young or old, vitamin D is needed for a healthy nervous system. Our blood does a better job of clotting. Our teeth are strong and healthy. And our outlook is sunny!

Where can we find it? Other than the sunlight, fatty fish and sunflower seeds are the only sources.

What happens if you don't get enough? You won't absorb calcium and phosphorus well and will, therefore, run the risk of having those deficiencies. Rickets are a well-known, but now rare, form of improper bone formation, caused in part by too little vitamin D. Your thyroid gland needs vitamin D. Without the right amount, you could find yourself pretty flabby and sluggish.

What happens if you get too much? Too much D means too much calcium will be absorbed, which means not only possible hardening of the arteries but hardening of all your organs. This is a very rare development, highly unlikely to happen to you unless you take excessive amounts of vitamin D pills. Relatively minor symptoms of "overdosing" on vitamin D are a loss of coordination, tingling sensations in your hands and feet, and a possible sudden weight loss.

VITAMIN E, another fat soluble vitamin, has been in the news a lot in the past few years. Why? Mainly because it increases our stamina and endurance, gives new life to our cells, and protects us against pollution and environmental poisons. Because it strengthens the reproductive organs, some people feel it makes them "sexier." Because it helps prevent formation of scar tissue, vitamin E is believed by some to be a wonder vitamin for the skin—and a barrier against aging.

Where can we find it? Cold-pressed oils (especially wheat germ oil), egg yolk, seeds, nuts, and soybeans are the primary sources, although many foods, particularly whole grains, contain some.

What happens if you don't get enough? A vitamin E deficiency can show up in anemia, muscle and tissue shrinkage, and poor hemoglobin production.

What happens if you get too much? No problem with food, but massive doses of vitamin E can affect the body's chemistry, especially the production of hormones.

VITAMIN K is a fat soluble vitamin whose principal function is that it helps your blood to clot.

Where can we find it? Vitamin K is present in many foods, but the very best sources are cabbage, cauliflower, spinach and other leafy vegetables, soybeans, and pork liver.

What happens if you don't get enough? You might bleed excessively if you cut yourself, had a tooth pulled, or had an operation. However, most people absorb enough K through normal diet and digestion, and a deficiency is rare.

What happens if you get too much? Too much vitamin K can poison your system; that is, it can be toxic. For this reason, the sale of vitamin K is regulated by law and it is not available without a doctor's prescription.

CALCIUM, as discussed earlier, is important for the formation of our teeth and bones. It helps our wounds heal quickly. The clotting—even the flow— of our blood also is regulated by calcium.

Where can we find it? Most whole foods contain some calcium. Our major sources are dark green vegetables, dried beans, soybeans, sea vegetables, Cheddar cheese, fish and other seafood, and seeds— particularly unhulled sesame seeds.

What if we don't get enough? We could suffer from porous, brittle, and badly-shaped bones, and from tooth decay. Other signs of calcium deficiency are nervousness, little tolerance for pain, leg cramps, and constipation.

What happens if we get too much? That does not seem to be much of a problem unless you get too much from dairy products; that would increase your need for calcium, and could lead to a possible deficiency.

PHOSPHORUS helps calcium with your bone and tooth formation and aids your muscles and nerves in their functions.

Where can we find it? The same foods that contain calcium also have phosphorus. Nuts and whole grains, cranberries, and red cabbage are other good sources.

What happens if you don't get enough? When you do not get enough phosphorus your body loses calcium, giving you the deficiency symptoms of a low calcium intake. You could also feel weak and sluggish, both physically and mentally.

What happens if you get too much? It is extremely unusual for anyone to take in too much phosphorus.

MAGNESIUM is another good friend to your bones and teeth. It activates a large percentage of your body's enzymes, especially those that build and synthesize protein. A minor benefit—a "social" benefit, primarily—of magnesium is to reduce the body odors and bad breath that rise from dental problems.

Where can we find it? Green leafy vegetables, dried beans and peas, peanuts, nuts, whole grains—especially buckwheat and wheat—are the best sources.

What happens if you don't get enough? Magnesium is especially important for kids. If your diet is short of magnesium your physical growth slows down and your ability to learn is lessened. Some kids who are restless, who become known as troublemakers in school, are found to have magnesium deficiencies.

What happens if you get too much? If you take too many vitamin pills or supplements that include magnesium, you could have diarrhea for a while. If you eat too many whole foods rich in magnesium, the worst that will happen is a stomach ache.

POTASSIUM does for your heart and nerves what calcium, phosphorus, and magnesium do for your bones and teeth. It gets together with phosphorus to send oxygen to your brain and with magnesium to synthesize protein. Potassium maintains the water balance in your tissues and helps to regulate the blood flow, keeping the blood pressure at an even level.

Where can we find it? Fruits and vegetables are excellent sources. Dried beans and meats are good suppliers, too.

What happens if you don't get enough? People of all ages who don't eat enough fruit and vegetables tend to be bothered by a lot of minor problems; for example, headaches, constipation or diarrhea, colds, acne, and an inability to think clearly (not such a minor problem when you're in school!)

What happens if you have too much? Although this is unusual, symptoms of too much potassium can be the same as those for too little potassium.

IRON is essential for building hemoglobin in your blood and supplying some of the enzymes needed to provide energy.

Where can we find it? Iron is present in most natural foods, but it is still difficult to get as much as you need if you are female—a grown woman, a teenager, or a sub-teenager. The best foods, other than liver and red meats, are dried beans, whole grains, dark green vegetables, apricots, sunflower seeds, egg yolk, and seafood.

What happens if you don't get enough? Anemia is the biggest problem. All the problems associated with anemia—fatigue, poor resistance to infection, shortness of breath, and others—can occur. Foods rich in vitamin C and the B Complex vitamins help you absorb iron. Foods rich in vitamin E (or vitamin E supplements), when eaten at the same time as iron-rich foods, make it difficult for your body to absorb iron easily.

What happens if you get too much? Too much iron is very rare, especially in girls and women.

CHLORINE is the body's built-in housekeeper. All the toxic substances and waste in your body are whisked through your system with the help of chlorine. This mineral also aids in the digestion of protein.

Where can we find it? Animal products, salt, leafy green vegetables, and seafood are very good chlorine-containing foods.

What happens if you don't get enough? A chlorine shortage can retard your growth. People with too little chlorine often feel nervous, anxious, and disinterested in life.

What happens if you get too much? This would be such an unusual situation that it really is not a matter for your concern.

SODIUM, otherwise known as salt, plays a major role in maintaining an even water balance in your body. It also has a steadying effect on your nervous system.

Where can we find it? Just about all foods, other than fruit, contain sodium. Seafood, animal products, and processed food are some of the major suppliers.

What happens if you don't get enough? Fatigue, muscle cramps, lack of appetite and a general disinterest in life are common signs.

What happens if you get too much? This is more common than a deficiency. Water retention, acne, and high blood pressure are some signs of a sodium overload.

FLUORINE seems to contribute to the health of your bones and teeth. It also helps the general condition of your cells and blood.

Where can we find it? Seafood, brown rice, onions, and some other vegetables contain fluorine. Water which has been treated with fluoride is a source of chemical fluorine.

What happens if you don't get enough? More tooth decay!

What happens if you get too much? One problem with drinking fluoridated water is the large amount of fluorine you swallow. Symptoms of an excess of fluorine include mottled teeth and some disruptions of the nervous system.

IODINE is needed in very tiny amounts only. Even so, the absence of it would cause death. Iodine enables your thyroid gland to function properly.

Where can we find it? Seafood, sea vegetables, garlic, dairy products, and many fruits and vegetables contain iodine.

What happens if you don't get enough? An iodine deficiency can cause goiter, an enlarged thyroid gland, or reduced secretion by the thyroid gland. When the thyroid gland is not functioning well, you are apt to be overweight and sluggish, and find it hard to think clearly.

What happens if you get too much? Too much iodine also causes the thyroid gland to slow down.

There are a number of other vitamins and minerals that are important, but are not considered to be among the major nutrients your body requires. Let's take a brief look at each of them.

INOSITOL, another B vitamin, helps prevent hardening of the arteries, helps protect many of your vital organs, and helps you keep your healthy, good looks. Liver and brewers yeast are excellent sources, whole grains and citrus fruits very good.

PABA, also a B vitamin, stimulates bacteria in your intestines, helps you use protein more efficiently, builds your red blood cells, and contributes to the health of your skin. The only known good sources are liver, wheat germ, brewers yeast, sunflower seeds, milk, and beef.

PANTOTHENIC ACID, the final B vitamin, helps produce cortisone and therefore is considered important in stimulating your adrenal glands and in fighting arthritis. There are many sources, including egg yolk, organ meats, whole grains, brewers yeast, rice, sunflower seeds, soybeans and corn.

ZINC is essential for a number of enzymes needed for digestion and energy production. It also helps you utilize the B Complex vitamins. It is plentifully available in shellfish, liver, wheat germ, and whole grains.

COPPER helps you absorb iron and therefore helps prevent anemia. It is contained in most natural whole foods and in much of our drinking water. Dried beans, seafood, whole grains, almonds, apricots, and egg yolk are other good sources.

SELENIUM assists vitamin E in its functions. Animal products, whole grains (especially rice), and vegetables (particularly onions and garlic) are most rich in selenium.

SULFUR helps your blood resist disease and strengthens your hair, skin, and nails. All foods which contain protein contain substantial amounts of sulfur; for example, green leafy vegetables and carrots.

MANGANESE helps to produce enzymes that synthesize fat. Whole grains, dried beans, and nuts are the best sources. Fruits, especially blueberries, also are good.

CHROMIUM is important because it metabolizes glucose for energy. Whole grains, vegetable oils, animal fats, and some seafood are good sources.

SILICON, VANADIUM, TIN, and **NICKEL** are known as trace minerals. While tests have shown they are necessary for good health in animals, little is known about their contribution to the health of humans.

Foods to Stay Away From

Some foods are recognized by just about all the experts to be downright bad for us. Many of these so-called "bad" foods contribute to the biggest problem many people have in this country—the overeating of food with more calories than nutrients. If you are between ten and the high teens, this especially applies to your age group.

It is really unfortunate that we humans have such a taste for sugary, white flour foods. In tests with mice and rats, scientists have discovered that animals on a healthy diet, one that meets all their nutrition needs, don't eat as many sweets as those whose diet is deficient. Why? I explained earlier how white sugar raises, then drops, our blood sugar—but that is not all it does to us. Sugar needs the B vitamins in order to be digested. Most foods, such as other carbohydrates, contain enough of these vitamins to ensure a smooth digestion. *Sugar does not.* Imagine you have just had something sugary. In order for it to be digested by your body, sugar "eats up" all of the B vitamins already in your intestinal tract. The next time you eat something—the next meal or a snack in between—your body doesn't have those necessary B vitamins ready to aid digestion.

Without any of the surrounding vitamins, minerals, and enzymes that usually come with our intake of natural sugar (that found in grains, vegetables, and fruits), *sucrose*—white sugar—is basically a *"pure" drug.* That explains why we find ourselves so addicted to it. Sugar does satisfy your appetite, but only briefly, and artificially. Your desire for sugar, and other nutritionally useless foods, will return as soon as your blood sugar drops again. And because sugar destroys your B vitamins, the symptoms of B vitamin deficiencies develop.

Sugar also disrupts the calcium-phosphorus balance we talked of before. Your brain relies on the level of your blood sugar to function smoothly. When your blood sugar levels jump up and down, your emotions will, too! You'll find that a kid (maybe you, sometimes) who can't make up her or his mind probably just finished a candy bar!

If you do eat sugary foods, try to precede them with a balanced meal first. Earn that treat (I know they taste good!) by giving your body what it needs first. Your system still won't be too thrilled by your intake of white sugar, especially if you overdo (*you* wouldn't do that), but at least the effects of the sugar will be less noticeable in a well-nourished body.

Another heavyweight contributor to bad nutrition is white flour. Scientists have done a study for this substance, too. One group of rats was put on an exciting diet of *only* enriched white bread for three months. By the end of this period, two-thirds of the rats had died. The remaining one-third had become shrunken in size, and often deformed. Of course, this is an extreme example. No kid would try to live on just enriched white bread—and no mom would let him. But the results of this test, and others, do seem to indicate that enriched white bread should be eaten in moderate amounts—at the most.

What is enriched white bread? This is bread made from white flour, flour that has had the germ of the wheat—which includes most of the nutrients—removed. This flour is then "enriched" by adding four synthetic vitamins (thiamine, riboflavin, niacin, and iron) to replace these and a dozen other vitamins that are naturally present in wheat germ. White flour, like sugar, also needs the B vitamins to aid its digestion; as you can see, it contains only three of them.

What else is wrong with white flour? Nutritionists and other scientists think that many of the ailments of modern man and woman have white flour as their principal cause. While many of us can digest whole grains easily, not all of us have the same success with heavily processed products. Is it the lack of fiber and vitamins? Is it the long list of chemicals added to many enriched-flour baked goods—chemicals added to bleach the flour, to kill fungi, to prevent staleness, to keep the product "squeezable" and light? Symptoms as minor as a cold and as serious as cancer and heart disease have been linked to white flour.

Sugar and white flour are not the only two foods to be avoided or eaten in moderation. Salt and fat also are coming under attack more and more lately.

What can we say about salt that is good? Like most foods in their natural state, salt is beneficial to us. In fact, it is essential to our health. Each of us has the equivalent of a miniature ocean inside our bodies. Our blood and other body fluids have a salty content similar to that ocean. When we rely on our body's own wisdom, we know when we have had too much salt because we feel thirsty. Sometimes our bodies can't handle the problems we create with our food intake—like eating too much salt—and then we get sick.

Some of the problems thought to be caused by too salty a diet involve vital organs, like your kidneys and your heart. Your kidneys, which have the job of pumping salt into your blood, are probably under the most constant attack by salt. After your kidneys get that salt out, and into the blood stream, they reabsorb the salt again and the same process starts all over again. The heart is involved because salt—too much of it—raises your blood pressure, forcing more liquid into your bloodstream and causing your heart to work harder.

Too much salt will cause you to retain too much fluid in your body. What happens then? Well, for one thing, the newest findings related to water retention are helpful to you girls who have begun menstruating. Water retention has been found to play a large part in causing cramps and bloating. People trying to lose weight, or those whose weight mysteriously shoots up and slides down can help stabilize their weight by cutting out salt. Research also shows that depression and sharp swings in mood—*very* happy one minute, *very* unhappy the next—can be traced to salt retention.

We really do not need to add salt to our foods. All foods have some salt, and some, like meats, some vegetables and fruits, soy sauce, pickles, seafood, and sea vegetables are very high in salt. The salt you buy in the supermarket is complete with additives to ensure a smooth flow. Like sugar, salt is addictive, and the people who really crave it the most are the very ones whose bodies need it the least. If you do continue to use salt, use only sea salt, and try to use it intelligently.

And what about fat? Whoever heard very much good about fat? Nevertheless, it has a place—however small—in our diets. Without fats, we wouldn't have a source of fatty acids, our foods wouldn't be digested so quickly, we would always feel hungry, and we would not be able to maintain an even body temperature of 98.6°.

But as a nation that depends on animal protein for much of its diet, we have been found to suffer undesirable side effects from eating too much animal fat. Fat from animal sources, like meat, butter, and eggs, is chemically saturated. In other words, it contains many hydrogen atoms. This type of fat is called saturated fat, and it is thought to contain cholesterol. When you have too much cholesterol in your body, your bloodstream—your arteries and capillaries—can get clogged up, making it difficult for the blood to get to and from your heart. This can be a cause of heart attacks. Of course, it is *very rare* for a kid like yourself to have a heart attack, but children as young as two have been found to have cholesterol blocking their bloodstreams. That could be a major problem later in your life. Of course, many years before you probably would face any chance of heart or arterial disease, fat would very likely make you fat if you eat too much of it!

The fat in vegetable products is called unsaturated fat and is better for you. Some of these foods are nuts, peanuts, seeds, and oils from vegetables, such as corn, safflower, or soy oil. Coconuts are one source of vegetable fat that is saturated. Fish and poultry are two sources of animal fat that do not contain high levels of cholesterol. Eating an unrefined diet high in bulk will help by absorbing some of the fatty particles and allowing them to be eliminated as waste. Remember we mentioned how easily chemicals and other toxic substances lodge in fat? That's just one more reason to cut back on the animal fat you consume.

What other foods may not be contributing to your health? Citrus fruits, such as oranges, grapefruit, and lemons, have long been considered valuable because of their vitamin C content. However, recent research findings indicate that *very heavy* consumption of citrus fruits may bring on the very symptoms of a vitamin C deficiency they supposedly cure; for example, frequent colds, headaches, and unusual fatigue. Citrus fruits, especially oranges, have always been one of the most common allergic foods. What is an allergy? We haven't talked about that so far. The word allergy means an unusual response to what is normally a harmless substance; in this case, a food.

Do you have food allergies? If you and your parents believe you are eating a good, balanced diet, but you still don't feel so great some of the time—upset stomach, diarrhea, feeling nervous and upset, not doing as well in school as you should be—maybe you should have a doctor check you for possible food allergies. My son is not as old as you are, but he really has food allergy problems if we don't watch what he eats (that's a fulltime job; he's *always* eating!)

New research has shown that a food can destroy your white blood cells if you are allergic to that food. What happens is this: An allergic person does not digest the food well so tiny pieces of the food pass into the bloodstream through the tissue walls. Once the food is in your bloodstream all parts of your body may be affected, from headaches or mental confusion to swollen ankles and clumsy feet. Since your white blood cells normally have the job of keeping invaders (like viruses and germs) under control, they aren't accustomed to having this job of coping with allergic invasions, too! Now they have to struggle to keep out the little offending particles of food as well. What happens often, if you have this problem, is that you get sick more easily; while the white blood cells are tearing around, trying to control the allergy problems, those germs are sneaking in.

All the possible symptoms for allergy would take too long to list here. If you think you may be bothered by a food allergy, do some thinking about what you eat and how you feel afterward. If you are a genius at school in the morning, but maybe not so bright in the afternoon, maybe something you have for lunch (milk, maybe?) isn't helping. A good place to begin checking is with foods that you really love. These are the ones most likely to be causing problems. Naturally this doesn't mean foods that just taste good to you, only those you feel you *must* have.

Super Foods for Better Nutrition

Keeping in mind that each of us is at least a little different from everyone else, let's get to some foods that are especially deserving of attention—at least by most of us. I call them...**THE SUPER FOODS!**

What are super foods? They are those foods that, bite for bite, give us more than their share of nutrients. Soybeans head the list. These tough little beans have been a staple in many countries, China and Japan, for example, for thousands of years. We are finally discovering, with a lot of excitement, how much the soybean has to offer us in this country. The soybean is the only vegetable that can rival the protein content of meat. Soybeans also contain large amounts of vitamins and minerals that animal sources do not give you, such as the B Complex vitamins and lecithin, and they give you these "bonuses" without saturated fat. Soybeans have a higher calcium content than milk, more iron than spinach, and more potassium than bananas. Taken with grains, they form a complete protein, providing the amino acids most often lacking in grains (lysine).

Products made from the soybean can replace such animal products as milk, eggs, and meat in cooking and baking. In the recipe section of this book you will find plenty of enjoyable and nutritious uses for tofu, tempeh, soy sauce, and miso. What are these foods? Tofu, often called bean curd because of its resemblance to cottage cheese, is a white creamy substance made from soymilk. It works very well as a substitute for eggs, cream, and cheese in cooking. Many kids who have tried it like tempeh for its resemblance to hamburgers. Tempeh is made from fermented soybeans which are molded into small patties or cakes and then cooked like hamburgers. Soy sauce is found in two forms; tamari sauce and shoyu. Tamari is made only from aged and fermented soybeans into a liquid that is used for seasoning and cooking. Shoyu is made from both soybeans and wheat in a similar process. Most of the soy sauce sold in this country is shoyu, mislabeled as tamari. In the recipes in this book I have called it tamari, because that is what most of us are used to seeing on the labels. However, you can use either shoyu or tamari in the recipes (shoyu is not as strong in flavor as tamari, so you may need to adjust the amount you use to your taste).

Miso is a thick and creamy paste that may be light brown to nearly black depending on what other foods are included. Some miso is pure soy; others have barley, rice, or koji added. All are really tasty as sandwich spreads, in soups, or as seasonings. Try 'em . . . you'll like 'em!

People who eliminate animal food from their diets should eat some fermented soy foods daily. They are the only vegetable sources of vitamin B_{12}, other than sea vegetables—which themselves are a potent source of vitamins and minerals.

Seeds are still another source of nutrient-rich food power. Sesame seeds contain more calcium than milk and make a good substitute for that food. In addition to their high calcium content, seeds offer substantial amounts of protein and the B vitamins, minerals such as phosphorus, potassium, magnesium, and zinc, and unsaturated fatty acids. Tahini, a creamy "butter" made from sesame seeds, is tasty as a sandwich spread or as an ingredient in many recipes. Sesame seeds combined with wheat and soybeans provide an excellent protein source, as do sesame and rice.

Sunflower seeds are also nutritional nuggets. Not only do they offer the B Complex vitamins and minerals of sesame seeds, they are as much as fifty per cent (50%) protein. They have a high iron content and are an excellent source of vitamins D and E.

No matter how old you were on your last birthday, you have learned already that life is full of choices. As you get older, you'll find that the choices you decide on—the decisions you make—will become more important. It is hard for me to think of any choices that will be more important to you than how you decide to take care of yourself. An awfully important part of "taking care of yourself" has to do with what you put into your body. If you have read this book with some care and interest, you know that I believe that we do best for our bodies by cutting down the amount of animal foods in our diet; getting the nutrients that meat, eggs, and milk provide from other sources. Many qualified nutritionists support that point of view.

Beginner's Basics

Congratulations! You made it to the recipe section (*really* reading everything along the way, I hope).
That tells me a couple of things about you:
One, you're ready to start cooking.
Two, you're starving from all that reading!
One great thing about food is that we all share it. So get ready to show your stuff—then pass it around!

Before you begin . . .
You'll find your way through the upcoming recipes more easily if you read through a few tips first. Check the next few pages for cooking instructions and terms. If you get stuck in the middle of a recipe, just shuffle back and check 'em again.

Notice the symbols next to each recipe:

 means "easy as pie"

 means "takes more time and concentration"

 means "call a friend or parent to help if you are new to cooking"

* means to check the Food Dictionary on page 168 if you are not familiar with the ingredient listed

KITCHEN MATH

Measurements to Know

If the recipe says this:	It means this:
Pinch	Less than ⅛ teaspoon
3 teaspoons	1 tablespoon
4 tablespoons	¼ cup
8 tablespoons	½ cup
12 tablespoons	¾ cup
1 cup (liquid)	½ pint
2 cups (liquid)	1 pint
4 cups (liquid)	1 quart
2 pints	1 quart
4 quarts	1 gallon
16 ounces	1 pound

Better Nutrition Substitutions

If you don't like to use this:	You can use this:
1 tablespoon baking powder	1 teaspoon baking soda plus 2 teaspoons cream of tartar
½ cup butter or margarine	⅓ cup oil
1 cup butter or margarine	⅔ cup oil
1 tablespoon dry yeast	1 cake fresh yeast
2 tablespoons flour for thickening	1 tablespoon arrowroot *or* cornstarch
1 1-ounce square unsweetened chocolate	¼ cup carob *or* cocoa plus 1 teaspoon oil
½ teaspoon powdered ginger	1 tablespoon grated fresh gingerroot
1 cup sugar	¾ cup honey† *or* 1¼ cups maple syrup†
1 cup white flour	1 cup less 2 tablespoons whole-wheat flour
1 cup catsup	¾ cup tomato sauce plus ¼ cup maple syrup plus 2 tablespoons vinegar
1 cup milk	1 cup soymilk (see page 55), apple juice, water, vegetable broth, *or* squash "milk" (see page 55)

†When substituting honey or maple syrup for sugar, reduce the amount of the other liquids called for in the recipe. Reduce by ¼ cup for each cup of sugar you replace. When you use honey, you should also lower the oven temperature by 25 degrees to prevent overbrowning.

KITCHEN VOCABULARY

Bake means to cook in a hot oven.

Baste means to spoon some of the liquid in the pan back over the food while it is cooking.

Beat means to stir hard with a spoon or an electric mixer.

Blend means to mix two or more ingredients together until smooth.

Boil means to have lots of bubbles on the surface of your cooking liquid. Water boils at 212 degrees.

Broil means to cook in the broiler section of your oven. Set the oven's temperature control knob to "broil."

Brush means to use a pastry brush or large clean paint brush to cover your food with oil, glaze, egg or whatever is called for in the recipe.

Chop means to cut your food into uneven pieces of about the same size with a heavy knife or food chopper.

Coat means to cover or roll your food in flour, crumbs or whatever is called for in the recipe.

Cube means to cut in small (¼ – ½ inch) squares with a knife or scissors.

Cut in margarine or oil means to blend it into your dry ingredients with a pastry blender or with two dull knives (crisscrossing each other).

Dice means to cut into tiny (⅛ – ¼ inch) squares with your knife or scissors.

Fold means to mix in your ingredient very gently with a whisk or wooden spoon. Use a folding motion, bringing your spoon down through the mixture and across the bottom, then up and over so that the ingredients on the bottom end up on top.

Fry means to cook in hot oil or fat.

Grate means to rub your food over a grater to make tiny shreds of food.

Grease means to rub the surface with oil or fat. A crumpled paper towel or a piece of waxed paper works well for doing this.

Mince means to chop into very small (¹⁄₁₆ – ⅛ inch) pieces with a heavy knife or chopper-in-bowl.

Pare means to take the skin off fruits or vegetables with a parer or small, sharp knife.

Preheat means to turn the oven on about 10 minutes before putting your food in.

Purée means to turn the whole food into a smooth mixture, usually using a food blender.

Sauté means to cook in a small amount of oil or margarine, usually in a frying pan.

Season means to add salt, herbs, or spices.

Sift means to put your flour through a sifter or fine mesh strainer to make it lighter.

Simmer means to cook just lower than the boiling point. Small bubbles will rise to the surface.

Sliver means to cut into long, skinny pieces.

Slice means to cut into even pieces, usually about ⅛ inch wide.

Steam means to cook on a rack or steamer over boiling water in a covered pan or in a double boiler over boiling water. The boiling water makes steam that cooks the food.

Stir means to blend until ingredients are well mixed. With a spoon, stir in circles.

Stir-fry means to sauté in a small amount of oil at high heat in a frying pan, stirring constantly.

KITCHEN KNOW-HOW

How to measure dry ingredients:

1. Always use a set of graduated measuring cups or spoons.
2. Fill the cup or spoon to overflowing. Drag the flat edge of a dull knife or spatula over the top to make it level.

How to measure liquid ingredients:

1. Always use a measuring cup, usually glass or plastic, whose rim is above the cup line markings so that you can measure accurately without spilling.
2. Put the measuring cup on a level counter. Stoop down so that your eye level is right in front of the measurement you need. Now pour in the ingredient until the desired measuring line is reached.

How to cook beans:

1. Early in the morning (or the night before), pour 1 pound (2 cups) of beans into a colander. Wash well under cold, running water.
2. Dump the beans into a large saucepan or Dutch oven. Cover with 6 cups of water. Swish the beans around, taking out any broken or shriveled beans, pebbles, or clumps of dirt.
3. Cover the pan. Let soak at least 6 hours or overnight.
4. Drain off the water by dumping the beans in a colander.
5. Pour 6 cups of fresh water over the beans. Don't add salt. (It toughens the beans!)
6. Cover the pan and put it on the burner. Bring to a boil. Reduce the heat and let simmer for the amount of time shown on the chart that follows.

BEAN BRAIN BOX

Soak first?	Use 2 cups† of these beans:	with this much liquid:	Cook this long:
No	Adzuki beans	1″ over top of beans	2–2¼ hours
Yes	Black-Eyed Peas	6 cups	1–1½ hours
Yes	Chick Peas	6 cups	2–2½ hours
Yes	Great Northern Beans	6 cups	2–2½ hours
Yes	Kidney Beans	6 cups	2 hours
No	Lentils	1″ over top of beans	40–45 minutes
Yes	Lima Beans	6 cups	2 hours
Yes	Navy Beans	6 cups	2 hours
Yes	Pea Beans	6 cups	2 hours
Yes	Pinto Beans	6 cups	1½–2 hours
Yes	Soybeans	6 cups	2–3 hours
No	Split Peas	1″ over top of beans	35–40 minutes

†Yes, you can cook 1 cup, 3 cups, or however many beans you have! Just add enough water to cover them by about 2 inches. You can also save time by cooking them in a pressure cooker but ask an experienced cook for help.

How to cook grains:

1. Get a heavy saucepan or frying pan and put in the amount of fresh water called for in the chart that follows.
2. Bring the water to a boil.
3. Very slowly sprinkle in the grain. Try not to let the water stop boiling. Don't add salt.
4. Put the lid on the pan and lower the heat. Simmer gently for the length of time shown on the chart.

or:

1. Get a heavy saucepan or frying pan. Pour in 1 or 2 tablespoons of oil.
2. Turn the heat on to medium high.
3. Dump in the grain. Stir-fry for a few minutes until coated with oil and as golden brown as you would like.
4. Pour in the amount of water called for and bring to a fast boil on high heat. Do this carefully as steam will rise when you add the water.
5. Cover the pan, lower the heat, and simmer for 5 or 10 minutes *less* than the time called for on the chart.

GRAIN BRAIN BOX

Use 1 cup of this grain:	with this much liquid:	Cook this long:
Barley	2½ cups	45–60 minutes
Brown Rice	2–2½ cups	45–60 minutes
Bulgur (Cracked Wheat)	2 cups	20 minutes
Cornmeal	1 cup	15 minutes
Couscous	2 cups	10–15 minutes
Kasha (Buckwheat groats)	2 cups	15 minutes
Millet	2½–3 cups	40–50 minutes
Oatmeal	2 cups	5–15 minutes
Rolled Rye	3 cups	15–20 minutes
Soy Grits	2 cups	15 minutes
Whole-wheat berries	2½–3 cups	60–70 minutes

How to cut onions (and other vegetables):

1. Use a cutting board.
2. Cut the onion in half through the root ends. Cut off tiny slivers from root ends. Peel off the skin with the tip of your knife or with your fingers.
3. To chop onions, cut onion halves into ¼–½-inch slices. Pile the slices on the cutting board. Using a large chopping knife, hold the tip of the knife down with the palm of your left hand (if you are right handed). With your right hand, hold the knife handle. Now bring the knife up and down and back and forth over the onions until they are all chopped.
4. To mince onions, cut off tiny slivers from root ends. Peel off skin. Cut onion in ⅛–¼-inch slices. Make piles of several slices each, then cut ⅛-inch slices in one direction. Hold the slices together (carefully) and cut ⅛-inch slices going in the other direction.
5. To slice onions into crescents, cut the onion in half through the root ends. Peel off the skin. Make cuts of desired thickness through the root ends. Cut thin slivers off ends and separate into crescents.
6. To slice onions into rings, cut off the root ends and peel off the skin. Make cuts of desired thickness. Separate into rings.

How to make bread crumbs:

1. To make fresh bread crumbs, trim the crusts from fresh bread. Rub each slice of bread between your fingers until it crumbles into small bits. Pack loosely into a measuring cup to measure.
2. To make dry bread crumbs, use stale bread or put slices of bread on a cookie sheet and allow to dry in oven with the temperature set at 250 degrees. Leave in oven about 30–60 minutes or until they are dried out but not brown.) Remove from oven and break into pieces. Whiz the pieces in the blender until fine crumbs form *or* put in a small plastic bag and crush with a rolling pin until fine *or* rub against the fine or coarse side of a grater.

How to make substitutes for dairy milk:

1. To make Nut or Seed "milk," use a blender to liquify 2 ounces (⅓ – ½ cup) of sesame seeds, raw cashews, or blanched almonds with 6 ounces (¾ cup) of water. Good for making "milk" shakes.
2. To make Soy "milk," blend ¼ cup tofu* with ⅔ cup water in blender. Can be used for beverages or in baking.
3. To make Squash "milk," dice and remove the seeds from a medium-size yellow squash (but don't peel it). Measure 1¼ cups of the squash into blender jar. Pour in water just to cover the squash. Whirl in blender on high until smooth, about 1–2 minutes. Strain. Makes about 1 cup. Good for baking—especially in spice cake or pumpkin pie.

How to prepare tofu*:

1. Remove tofu from the water it was stored in and rinse under cold, running water. Place between two layers of paper towels and press gently to remove excess moisture. Then, slice, cube, or crumble it as the recipe directs and press it again between layers of paper towelling. Let stand for another 10–15 minutes until all excess moisture is removed.
2. Freezing tofu changes its texture and, for this reason, some recipes call for "frozen tofu." To freeze tofu, wrap in plastic wrap and store in the freezer for 2 or 3 days. (The color will darken and it will develop a meat-like texture.) When ready to use, thaw and drain before proceeding with recipe.

How to prepare and cook vegetables:

1. Wash vegetables well before cooking to remove any dirt or chemical residues that may be clinging to them. Scrub tough skinned vegetables energetically with a brush and wash leafy vegetables with several changes of cold water. If you are uncertain where they came from, you may want to peel or pare root vegetables. If you are not sure how much to cook, check the "How Much Is Enough?" guide on page 57.
2. To boil vegetables, add the prepared vegetables to a small amount of boiling, lightly salted water. When water returns to a boil, cover the pan and begin timing.
3. To steam vegetables, place a steamer basket in the bottom of pan. Add water to pan, keeping level of the water below the bottom of the steamer basket. Place vegetables in the steamer. Bring water to boil, cover pan tightly, and lower heat. Steam for the length of time shown on the chart that follows.

FRESH VEGETABLE COOKING GUIDE

To cook this vegetable:	Boil this long:	Or, steam this long:
Asparagus, spears	10–15 minutes	8–12 minutes
Asparagus, cut up	8–10 minutes	6–8 minutes
Beets, whole	35–60 minutes	30–40 minutes
Beets, sliced	15–20 minutes	8–10 minutes
Beet tops	5–10 minutes	3–6 minutes
Broccoli, stalks	15–20 minutes	8–10 minutes
Broccoli, flowerets	10–15 minutes	6–8 minutes
Cabbage, wedges	12–15 minutes	10–15 minutes
Carrots, sliced	15–20 minutes	10–15 minutes
Cauliflower, whole	20–25 minutes	20–30 minutes
Cauliflower, flowerets	10–15 minutes	12–15 minutes
Corn, cob	6–8 minutes†	5–6 minutes
Green Beans, cut up	15–25 minutes	7–10 minutes
Onions, small	22–35 minutes	14–16 minutes
Peas	8–15 minutes	6–8 minutes
Potatoes, whole	35–40 minutes	—
Potatoes, cut up	20–25 minutes	14–18 minutes
Pumpkin, cut up	30–40 minutes	—
Spinach	5–7 minutes	3–5 minutes
Squash, summer, sliced	15–20 minutes	8–10 minutes
Sweet potatoes, whole	30–40 minutes	—

†For corn on the cob, use a full pot of briskly boiling water.

HOW MUCH IS ENOUGH?

This much of this:	Will give you:
1 pound apples	3 medium apples
1 pound bananas	3 medium bananas
2 large or 3 small bananas	1 cup puréed banana
1 cup raw barley	3 cups cooked barley
1 cup dried beans	2–2½ cups cooked beans
1 pound bread	9 cups bread crumbs
1 slice bread	⅔ cup bread crumbs
1 pound broccoli	enough for 3 people
1 cup raw bulgur (cracked wheat)	2 cups cooked bulgur
1 pound cabbage	5–6 cups shredded cabbage
1 pound carrots	3½ cups sliced carrots
1 medium carrot	about ½ cup shredded carrot
1 head cauliflower	enough for 3–4 people
1 pound flour	2¾–3 cups sifted flour
1 cup raw kasha (buckwheat groats)	2 cups cooked kasha
1 lemon	3 tablespoons juice plus 1 tablespoon grated rind
2 cups elbow macaroni	4 cups cooked elbow macaroni
1 pound margarine (or butter)	2 cups margarine (or butter)
1 cup raw millet	2 cups cooked millet
1 pound mushrooms	5 cups sliced mushrooms
3 cups uncooked noodles	2 cups cooked noodles
1 pound onions	4 cups sliced or chopped onions
1 large onion	1 cup chopped onion
1 pound potatoes	2 cups sliced potatoes
1 pound oranges	2 large oranges
1 orange	⅓ cup juice plus 1–2 tablespoons grated rind
½ pound uncooked pasta (spaghetti)	3½ cups cooked pasta (enough for 3 people)
1 pound shelled peanuts or nuts	3 cups whole or chopped nuts
1 pound peanut or nut butter	1¾ cups nut butter
1 pound peaches	4–5 peaches
1 pound pears	2–3 pears
1 pound raisins	2½–3 cups
1 cup raw brown rice	2½ cups cooked rice
1 pound raw spinach	1 cup cooked spinach
1 pound tomatoes	4 tomatoes or 1½ cups chopped tomatoes
1 pound tofu	1¾–2 cups tofu
1 cup whole-wheat berries	1½ cups cooked whole-wheat berries

WHICH WHISK WHERE?

An illustrated guide to kitchen utensils.

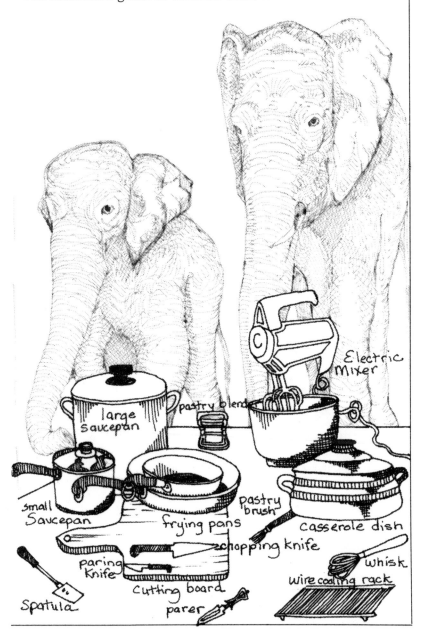

KITCHEN SAFETY

Cooking will be safer and a lot more fun if you follow some simple precautions. Accidents happen even to experienced adult cooks. If you are a beginner in the kitchen, try to start your cooking adventures when an adult is at home.

When preparing food:

1. Keep knives sharp and always use a cutting board with them.
2. Never throw a knife into a sink full of water. Put it aside to wash separately so that no one (especially you!) is accidentally cut.
3. When using a sharp knife, always cut *away* from your body.
4. When using an electric mixer or blender, always keep your hands away from any moving parts.
5. Never put a spoon or other utensil into the mixing bowl or blender while it is running. Always place lid on blender jar before turning on blender.
6. Keep appliance cords out of your way and unplug them when the appliance is not in use.

When cooking:

1. Dress for safety. If you have long hair, pin it back or put it up out of the way. Don't wear floppy sleeves or long flowing skirts.
2. Keep the oven and broiler clean so that grease and spilled food won't catch fire.
4. Use potholders!
5. Keep the handles on pans turned in on the stove so that you don't accidentally bump into them or catch your sleeve on them and cause a spill.
6. When taking the lids off pans of hot food, point them away from you to prevent burns from steam.

If an accident should happen:

1. If food in a pan catches on fire, turn off the heat and cover the pan with a lid. If food in the oven or broiler catches on fire, turn off the oven, keep the oven door closed, and call an adult to pour baking soda on top of the flames.
2. If your hair or clothes catch on fire, immediately fall to the floor and roll until the flames go out. Shout for help.
3. If you burn yourself, hold the burned area under cold running water for a minute or two. If red and blistered call an adult or a doctor.
4. If you cut yourself, hold a clean towel over the bleeding area until the bleeding stops. If the cut is too big for a Band-Aid, call an adult or a doctor!

READY . . .SET. . .GO . . .

Cooking will be more fun than frazzle if you follow these simple steps:
1. Wash your hands.
2. Read the recipe all the way through before you start.
3. Get out the pot, pans, and other utensils that you will need.
4. Put all the ingredients that you will need on the counter.
5. Do all your washing, chopping or slicing, and measuring before you start to cook.
6. Clean up your mess as you go along.
7. COOK WITH A HAPPY HEART!

Warm-ups

The chances are good that you are a "breakfast skipper." Once kids are old enough to make their own choices, this is one they often make.

It's an easy choice—easier than making breakfast! But consider your trusty body. Your appestat† may be sleeping at night but your body is working harder than ever—working hard to rebuild the many cells in your body that carry you through your active days.

Give yourself a break...fast. It can be quick, easy, and delicious and provide the nutrients your body needs to zap up your brain waves until lunch. Breakfast can even help keep you slim. Research shows that eating smaller meals more often helps to regulate your weight. When you wait until lunch or dinner to eat, your body thinks it is being starved and holds on to those calories—just in case tomorrow is going to be just as bad!

†The appestat is a mechanism in your body that tells you when you need to eat. A nutritious diet helps regulate your appestat, while a diet of junk food confuses it.

GOOD MORNING ENERGY

Get these ingredients ready:

2 cups leftover cooked rice
1 cup currants
1 cup water
½ cup tofu*
2 tablespoons barley malt* *or* rice syrup*

Now follow these steps:

1. Preheat oven to 350 degrees.
2. Place tofu and water in blender and blend until smooth. Mix tofu with all remaining ingredients and pour into a greased casserole. Cover.
3. Bake 35 minutes. Serve warm or at room temperature.

BERRY EARLY BULGUR

Get these ingredients ready:

½ cup bulgur*
2½ cups water
½ teaspoon vanilla
1 tablespoon maple syrup
½ cup blueberries

Now follow these steps:

1. Bring the water to a boil. Stir in the bulgur, vanilla, and maple syrup.
2. Cover and lower the heat to simmer. Simmer for 20 minutes, stirring every 5 minutes.
3. Stir in blueberries and serve with milk or soy milk.

COCK-A-DOODLE-DOO

Get these ingredients ready:

½ cup stone ground yellow corn meal
¼ teaspoon cinnamon
½ cup currants *or* raisins
2½ cups water

Now follow these steps:

1. Put the corn meal in a heavy, medium-size pan.
2. Slowly stir in water, being careful not to make lumps. Mix in the cinnamon and currants *or* raisins.
3. Bring the mixture to a boil, stirring constantly. Lower the heat to simmer; cook for 10 minutes, stirring often.

HONEY ALMOND GRANOLA

Get these ingredients ready:

7 cups rolled oats *or* rolled rye
1 cup wheat flakes
1 cup sunflower seeds
1 cup chopped almonds
½ cup coconut
½ cup sesame seeds
3 tablespoons oil
3 tablespoons honey

Now follow these steps:

1. Preheat oven to 350 degrees.
2. Mix all ingredients together in a large mixing bowl using a wooden spoon.
3. Spread on 2 cookie sheets.
4. Bake 25–30 minutes or until golden brown. (Check every few minutes after the first 20 minutes are up.)
5. Cool. Store in jars or other closed containers. Good plain or with nut milks.

JOSH'S TOFU PANCAKES

Get these ingredients ready:

¼ cup crumbled tofu*
1½ cups water
1 tablespoon maple syrup
1 teaspoon vanilla
¼ cup oil *or* melted margarine
1½ cups whole-wheat flour
1½ teaspoons baking powder

Now follow these steps:

1. Blend liquid ingredients in blender until smooth.
2. Mix flour and baking powder together in medium-size bowl. Stir in liquid ingredients, mixing in gently just until the dry ingredients are dampened.
3. Grease and heat a griddle or frying pan. Drop batter from a large spoon onto griddle, lightly spreading each cake with back of spoon to make a round cake. Cook until bottom of pancake is golden brown and edges of pancake begin to look dry. With spatula or pancake turner, loosen and turn cake; brown on other side.
4. Serve at once with maple syrup or apple butter.

APPLE-EGG FRENCH TOAST

Get these ingredients ready:

3 eggs
2 tablespoons maple syrup *or* honey
⅓ cup apple juice
8 slices whole-wheat bread

Now follow these steps:

1. Mix the eggs, maple syrup *or* honey, and apple juice together with an eggbeater or blender until well combined.
2. Pour the egg mixture into a large shallow pan. Place the bread slices in the pan in a single layer. Let soak for 5–10 minutes; turn the bread and soak on the other side for 5–10 minutes.
3. Grease and heat a griddle or frying pan. When hot, put as many bread slices as will fit into the pan and brown for about 4–5 minutes. Turn carefully with a spatula and brown the other sides in the same way, adding more grease if necessary. Repeat with remaining bread slices. Serve with maple syrup or warm apple butter sprinkled with toasted sunflower seeds. (Leftover Apple-Egg French Toast can be cooled, wrapped in plastic or aluminum foil, and frozen. Unwrap and reheat in a toaster or oven when needed.)

BAKED BANANAS

Get these ingredients ready:

    4 firm bananas
    2 tablespoons lemon juice
    1 tablespoon maple syrup
    1 cup Nutri-Grain Flaked Cereal

Now follow these steps:

1. Preheat oven to 350 degrees.
2. Peel the bananas.
3. Mix the lemon juice and maple syrup together in a shallow dish.
4. Roll each banana in the juice-syrup mixture.
5. Crush the cereal to about ⅔ cup and place on a plate. Roll each banana in the crumbs, then place in a shallow, greased baking pan.
6. Bake 20 minutes. Cool slightly before serving.

Naturally Good Tip: Try using scissors instead of a knife for many kitchen cut-ups. Dried fruit, herbs, scallions, fish fillets, and "trimming" burnt cakes or cookies are all likely subjects. For sticky foods, dip the scissors in water occasionally.

BAKED APPLE PANCAKE

Get these ingredients ready:

1 tablespoon margarine
3 cups peeled, cored, and sliced apples
½ teaspoon cinnamon
½ teaspoon allspice
Juice from ½ lemon
½ cup whole-wheat flour
¾ teaspoon baking powder
¼ cup honey
¼ cup yogurt* *or* crumbled tofu*
2 eggs

Now follow these steps:

1. Preheat oven to 400 degrees.
2. Melt the margarine in a large saucepan or frying pan.
3. Dump in the apples, cinnamon, allspice, and lemon juice. Mix gently. Cover pan. Turn heat to medium and bring to a boil. When boiling, turn heat to low and simmer, with the pan covered, for 10 minutes. Remove from heat.
4. Combine the flour and baking powder in a small mixing bowl. Pour in the honey, yogurt *or* tofu, and eggs. Mix with a fork just until smooth, about ½ minute.
5. Grease a 9-inch pie pan. Put about ⅓ of the batter in the bottom of the pie pan and spread around the bottom.
6. Bake for 5 minutes. Remove from oven.
7. Pour the apple mixture over the baked batter. Spoon the rest of the batter over the apples and spread evenly, making sure the batter touches the edges of the pan.
8. Bake 20–25 minutes. Cut in wedges (like a pie). Eat while hot.

CRUNCHY MUFFINS

Get these ingredients ready:

1½ cups rolled rye cereal flakes*
1 cup whole-wheat flour
2 teaspoons baking powder
½ teaspoon salt
⅔ cup water
⅓ cup vegetable oil
⅓ cup maple syrup
1 egg
½ cup raisins
½ cup sunflower seeds

Now follow these steps:

1. Preheat oven to 400 degrees.
2. Mix the first four ingredients together in a large bowl.
3. Mix remaining ingredients together in a small bowl. Dump all at once into the dry ingredients.
4. Mix gently, just until the dry ingredients are dampened.
5. Spoon into 12 greased or paper-lined muffin cups. (Cups will be about ⅔ full.)
6. Bake 15 minutes. Turn out onto wire rack and let cool slightly.

Naturally Good Tip: When making hard-cooked eggs, put the eggs in a pan with water to cover them. Bring to a rapid boil, cover, and remove pan from heat and let stand for 25–30 minutes. Drain and cool quickly under cold, running water.

OATMEAL BRAN MUFFINS

Get these ingredients ready:

1 cup oatmeal
1 cup bran *or* whole-wheat flour
1 tablespoon baking powder
1 teaspoon baking soda
½ teaspoon salt
1 egg
3 tablespoons oil
2 tablespoons barley malt* *or* molasses
1 cup soft tofu* *or* soy yogurt*
½ cup chopped nuts (preferably toasted)
½ cup currants or raisins

Now follow these steps:

1. Preheat oven to 425 degrees.
2. Put the oatmeal, bran *or* flour, baking powder, baking soda, and salt in a blender. Blend on high speed about 1 minute or until it looks like flour. Dump into a large mixing bowl.
3. Put all the remaining ingredients, *except the currants and nuts,* in the blender and blend about 1 minute or until smooth.
4. Pour the blended mixture over the oatmeal mixture and mix gently until all the dry ingredients are moistened. Stir in the nuts and currants *or* raisins.
5. Pour into greased or paper-lined muffin cups. (Cups will be about ¾ full.) Bake 15 minutes. Turn out onto wire rack to cool.

TERRIFIC TOASTIN' BREAD

Get these ingredients ready:

2 cups whole-wheat flour
2 cups cracked wheat flour
5 teaspoons baking powder
½ teaspoon salt
½ cup crumbled tofu*
½ cup sesame seeds
1½ cup water
3 tablespoons oil
1 tablespoon maple syrup *or* honey
  (add 1 or 2 more tablespoons for a sweeter bread)

Now follow these steps:

1. Preheat oven to 375 degrees.
2. Mix the flours, salt, and baking powder together in a medium bowl.
3. Put the water, tofu, oil, sesame seeds, maple syrup *or* honey in a blender. Blend on high for 1 minute.
4. Pour the blended ingredients over the flour mixture and mix with a wooden spoon until there aren't any dry specks showing, about 1 minute.
5. Grease a 9" × 5" × 3" bread pan. Spoon the batter in and smooth the top with a wet knife or clean, wet hands.
6. Bake 1 hour.
7. Remove to wire rack for 5 minutes. Take out of the pan and finish cooling. Good warm with apple butter or your favorite spread or cooled, sliced, and toasted!

APPLE BUTTER BREAD

Get these ingredients ready:

2¼ cups whole-wheat flour
1 tablespoon baking powder
1teaspoon cinnamon
½ teaspoon nutmeg
1 teaspoon salt
½ cup maple syrup
2 tablespoons soft margarine
3 eggs *or* 1 egg and ½ cup crumbled tofu*
1 cup apple butter
1 cup chopped nuts

Now follow these steps:

1. Preheat oven to 350 degrees.
2. Sift together the flour, baking powder, cinnamon, nutmeg, and salt into a large mixing bowl.
3. Add the maple syrup, margarine, eggs or egg and tofu, and apple butter. Mix with fork just until dry ingredients are dampened. Fold in the chopped nuts.
4. Pour into well greased 9″ × 5″ × 3″ bread pan. Let stand 10 minutes.
5. Bake 1 hour. Cool in pan for 10 minutes before turning out onto wire cooling rack to finish cooling.

YOGURT COFFEE CAKE

Get these ingredients ready:

    ¾ cup soft margarine
    1 cup maple syrup
    3 eggs
    2 teaspoons vanilla
    ½ cup honey
    2¾ cups whole-wheat flour
    2 teaspoons baking powder
    2 teaspoons baking soda
    ¼ teaspoon salt
    1⅓ cups plain yogurt*

    Filling: ⅓ cup maple syrup
             ¼ cup honey
             ¾ cup chopped walnuts
             2 teaspoons cinnamon

Now follow these steps:

1. Preheat oven to 350 degrees.
2. Grease a 10-inch tube pan well and dust with flour.
3. Mix the margarine, maple syrup, eggs, vanilla, and honey together in a large mixing bowl. Beat with an electric mixer on high speed for 2 minutes.
4. Mix the flour, baking powder, baking soda, and salt together in a small bowl.
5. Mix about ¼ of the flour mixture into the margarine mixture. Beat on low speed until blended.
6. Now mix about ⅓ of the yogurt into the margarine mixture until blended. Repeat until the flour mixture and yogurt are used up and everything is evenly blended.
7. Mix the Filling ingredients together in a small bowl.
8. Spoon ⅓ of the cake batter into the tube pan. Sprinkle with ⅓ of the Filling mixture. Repeat twice more.
9. Bake 1 hour. Let cool in pan on wire rack for 10 minutes. Remove from pan and finish cooling on wire rack.

KUCHICHA CAKE

Get these ingredients ready:

1½ cups maple syrup *or* ½ cup honey and 1 cup rice syrup*
1½ cups strongly brewed kuchicha tea (page 154)
½ cup mild oil
1½ cup raisins *or* chopped dried apricots
1 cup minced, washed but unpeeled apples
2½ cups whole-wheat flour
1 teaspoon baking soda
2 teaspoons baking powder
1 teaspoon cinnamon
1 teaspoon allspice
2 teaspoons grated fresh ginger
1 cup chopped walnuts *or* sunflower seeds

Now follow these steps:

1. Preheat oven to 350 degrees.
2. Mix together the sweeteners, kuchicha tea, oil, raisins or apricots, and apple in a medium saucepan. Bring to a boil over high heat, then lower heat and simmer for 10 minutes. Take off the burner and let cool to room temperature. (This can be left overnight if you need to.)
3. Mix all the remaining ingredients together in a large mixing bowl. Make an indentation in the center, then dump in the cooled ingredients.
4. Stir together well with a wooden spoon.
5. Pour into a well-greased and floured 10-inch tube pan.
6. Bake 1 hour. Check with a cake tester or toothpick. If the tester comes out dry, remove the cake from the oven. If not done, bake up to 20 minutes longer. Cool on wire rack for 10 minutes. Turn out of pan and finish cooling on wire rack.

SWEET PEAR ROLLS

Get these ingredients ready:

8 cups thinly sliced pears
1 6-ounce can frozen apple juice concentrate
1 tablespoon lemon juice
2 tablespoons arrowroot*
2 teaspoons apple pie spice *or* cinnamon
2 tablespoons water
½ package egg roll wrappers*

Now follow these steps:

1. Mix the pears, apple juice concentrate, and lemon juice together in a large frying pan or dutch oven. Bring to a boil, then lower heat and simmer for about 7 minutes.
2. Mix the arrowroot and spice in a small bowl, then slowly add the 2 tablespoons water, stirring to prevent lumps.
3. Now, stir this arrowroot mixture into the pear mixture. Continue cooking and stirring until thick and shiny looking.
4. Now start filling the egg roll wrappers. Each one gets ¼ cup of pear filling placed in the middle of the egg roll. Now fold together like an envelope and put aside on a waxed paper-covered plate or cookie sheet. When you have used up your egg rolls, you will still have filling left. (This will be used for topping; if you want you can make more egg rolls and serve them without topping.)
5. Now put ½-inch of any mild oil in a large frying pan (preferably cast iron) and heat to 375 degrees. (Use a frying/candy thermometer or drop a small ½-inch cube of bread into the hot oil to see how long it takes to turn golden brown and crispy. When that happens in a minute, you have the right temperature.)
6. Put in however many egg rolls will fit into the pan and still have a little space between them. Fry until they are golden on the bottom, about 2–4 minutes, adjusting heat as necessary to keep it at 375 degrees. Turn over with tongs and cook until the other side is also golden brown.

7. Put a layer of paper towels over a layer of newspaper. Take the egg rolls out of the pan with tongs and let them drain on the paper. Repeat these steps until you have used up the egg rolls.
8. Put the egg rolls on cookie sheets. Set the oven at 400 degrees and put the egg rolls in the oven for 10–15 minutes. Remove and serve plain or with the remaining pear mixture spooned over.

BREAKFAST SEED CAKES

Get these ingredients ready:

2 cups sunflower seeds
1 cup sesame seeds*
3 cups water
1 tablespoon maple syrup
½ cup whole-wheat flour
½ cup oil

Now follow these steps:

1. Put the seeds in a medium-size pan with the water. Cover and bring to a boil. Lower the heat and simmer for 1 hour.
2. Put half of the cooked seed mixture into a blender and whiz until somewhat broken up and blended. Pour into a medium-size bowl. Repeat with the remaining half.
3. Add maple syrup, whole-wheat flour, and 1 tablespoon of the oil; mix to form a stiff dough. With your hands, make 15 balls. (It will be easier to do if you wet your hands once in a while.) Now, flatten the balls into cakes with your hands or a rolling pin.
4. Put about half of the remaining oil in a heavy frying pan and heat on medium high until hot. Put 4–6 seed cakes in the pan and cook until golden. Turn and brown the other side. Add more oil whenever you need it. (You shouldn't need more than the ½ cup.) Repeat until all the seed cakes are cooked. Serve with maple syrup or applesauce.

Main Events

Each of us can help save food and energy by taking steps that may seem small but can add up to a more efficient use of our resources.

If we eat less animal protein and more vegetable protein, we can use foods that are closer to their natural state. Animal products and "convenience" foods take more energy using steps to be produced and shipped to us.

We can help by trying to cook only as much food as we need. And, if we cook too much, we can recycle our leftovers into new meals.

But, best of all, we can cook such delicious meals that nothing will be thrown away. So let's get our aprons on...

BARELY BEEF CHILI

Get these ingredients ready:

1 large onion, sliced
1 clove garlic, minced
2 tablespoons oil
½-pound lean ground beef
1 green pepper, chopped
1 28-ounce can tomatoes, chopped
1 teaspoon salt
1 bay leaf, crumbled
1 tablespoon chili powder
1 20-ounce can dark red kidney beans, drained
½ cup water

Now follow these steps:

1. Brown the onion and garlic in the oil.
2. Add beef and green pepper; brown, stirring as the meat cooks.
3. Add the tomatoes, salt, bay leaf, and chili powder. Cover and simmer over low heat for 2 hours.
4. Add the kidney beans and water. Heat. Serve over brown rice to complete the protein.

Naturally Good Tip: Need to fix that burned pot before your mom sees it? Pour about $\frac{1}{16}$-inch of water in the bottom of the pan, then sprinkle thickly with baking soda. Cover and sneak it into your room for 3 to 10 hours. (How BAD was it?) Now the burned portion should just peel off.

CHICKEN AND BROCCOLI STIR-FRY

Get these ingredients ready:

1 pound raw, boneless chicken
1 bunch broccoli
3 tablespoons oil
1 onion, sliced
1 clove garlic, minced
½ cup sliced celery
½ teaspoon salt
1½ teaspoons tamari sauce*
½ teaspoon Italian Seasoning *or* oregano
¼ cup water
1 tablespoon lemon juice

Now follow these steps:

1. Clean broccoli. Cut stems into ½-inch slices and separate flowerets.
2. Cut chicken into ½-inch strips.
3. Heat oil on medium heat in large frying pan or wok. Add the chicken and cook and stir for 5 minutes until lightly browned. Remove from the pan and put in a small bowl while you stir-fry the vegetables.
4. Add the broccoli, onions, celery, and garlic to the hot pan and cook and stir for 5 minutes.
5. Put the chicken back in the pan, along with the tamari, water, salt, and seasoning. Bring to a boil. Cover the pan, lower the heat, and simmer for 5 minutes. Check the chicken and broccoli for tenderness. If not tender, cook 5 minutes longer. Stir in the lemon juice. Serve over a grain or pasta.

CRUNCHY EGG ROLLS

Get these ingredients ready:

1 cup minced, cooked shrimp *or* chicken
2 tablespoons oil
1 cup cabbage, minced
1 cup minced celery
2 cups bean sprouts (preferably soy beans)
2 tablespoons tamari sauce*
1 tablespoon malt vinegar *or* mashed umeboshi plum*
1 tablespoon arrowroot*
3 tablespoons water
¼ teaspoon salt
12 egg roll wrappers*
Oil for cooking

Now follow these steps:

1. Heat the oil in a large frying pan or wok.
2. Dump in the onions and stir-fry on high heat for 1 minute.
3. Now dump in the cabbage, celery, and onions and continue to stir-fry for 1 more minute.
4. Add the shrimp *or* chicken and the bean sprouts, tamari sauce, malt vinegar *or* umeboshi plum, and salt. Lower the heat to medium and stir and cook for 1 minute longer.
5. Put the arrowroot in a cup and slowly stir in the water, making sure no lumps remain. Stir this mixture into the vegetable mixture and cook and stir until thick, about 1 minute. Remove from heat.
6. Remove one of the egg roll wrappers from the package. Put 2 level tablespoons of filling in the middle and then fold it up like an envelope. Put a small bowl of water by your side on the counter. After each "fold" of the egg roll, put a little water on with your fingers to glue it together. Repeat until you run out of filling, placing each egg roll on a cookie sheet or plate as it is finished.
7. Put about 1½-inch depth of oil in a heavy frying pan .or electric skillet and heat to 375 degrees. (Use a frying/candy

thermometer or drop a small ½-inch cube of bread into the hot oil to see how long it takes to turn golden brown and crispy. When that happens in a minute, you have the right temperature.) With a pair of tongs, *gently* lower 4 egg rolls, one at a time, into the hot oil. Count to 60 (slowly) and turn the egg rolls over with your tongs. Count to 60 again, remove and place on several layers of paper towels to drain while you finish cooking the rest. Continue in the same way until all the egg rolls are cooked. If you are not going to eat them right away, put them on a cookie sheet and keep in a 300 degree oven until ready.

CRABBY PIE

Get these ingredients ready:

1½ cups crumbled tofu*
½ cup water *or* vegetable broth
1 egg (optional)
½ teaspoon salt
¼ teaspoon pepper
2 tablespoons miso* *or* tamari sauce*
1 cup flaked crab meat
1 cup minced onion
2 tablespoons oil
½ cup chopped scallions
2 tablespoons sesame seeds
1 9-inch pie shell, prebaked for 5 minutes

Now follow these steps:

1. Preheat oven to 350 degrees.
2. Blend or beat tofu, liquid, egg (if used), salt, pepper, and miso *or* tamari sauce until smooth.
3. Sauté onions in oil for 5 minutes.
4. Combine tofu mixture with onions, crab meat, and scallions.
5. Pour into pie shell and sprinkle with sesame seeds.
6. Bake 30 minutes.

SASSY SCALLION FILLETS

Get these ingredients ready:

1 pound package frozen fish fillets
¼ teaspoon salt
¼ teaspoon pepper
1 tablespoon mayonnaise or Tofu Mayonnaise (page 164)
1 tablespoon prepared mustard
2 tablespoons chopped scallions

Now follow these steps:

1. Preheat broiler or broil unit of oven.
2. Place fish (still frozen) on rack of the broiler pan and sprinkle with salt and pepper.
3. Place pan in broiler or broil unit of oven so that top of fish is about 5 inches away from the heat source. Broil for 10 minutes. Turn block of fish over and broil 10 minutes on the other side. Remove from oven.
4. Mix together the mayonnaise or tofu mayonnaise, prepared mustard, and scallions. Spread over the fish.
5. Return to oven and broil for 2–3 minutes longer. Remove from oven, cut into serving size pieces and enjoy!

Naturally Good Tip: Here are some alternatives to stir-frying that leftover grain. Make "veggie burgers" or add it to puddings, soups, casseroles, breads, pancakes, or muffins. Or just reheat by piling into a greased baking dish, sprinkling with 1–2 tablespoons water and baking for 20–30 minutes. For a small amount, place in a strainer over boiling water and steam for a few minutes.

FISH IN ONION-MISO SAUCE

Get these ingredients ready:

1½ pounds fish fillets (your choice)
3 tablespoons oil
4 medium onions, sliced
2 tablespoons miso*
⅔ cup hot water
1 vegetable bouillon cube (optional)

Now follow these steps:

1. Preheat oven to 350 degrees.
2. Cook the onions in the oil in a large frying pan for 10 minutes on medium high heat; cover pan and lower heat to simmer. Simmer for about 45 minutes, checking once in a while and stirring if needed.
3. While the onions are cooking, grease a 7″×11″ shallow baking pan. Put in the fish and brush with a little oil. Bake 25 minutes.
4. When the onions are done, mix the miso with the hot water and bouillon cube (if using). Add the water a little at a time and stir until smooth. Mix into the onion mixture. Serve with the fish.

CRISPY FISH

Get these ingredients ready:

1 pound fish fillets
¾ cup Onion Tofu Dip (page 151)
1½ cups crushed Nutri-Grain Flaked Cereal
¼ cup oil or melted margarine

Now follow these steps:

1. Preheat oven to 400 degrees.
2. Pour Tofu Dip into pie pan or plate. Roll fish in dip until well covered.
3. Place crushed cereal on a piece of waxed paper. Roll fish in cereal until well coated with crumbs.
4. Place fish in shallow, greased casserole. Bake 20–25 minutes.

Naturally Good Tip: Onions that are stored in the refrigerator won't make you cry when you slice them!

BAKED CLAMS OREGANO

Get these ingredients ready:

3 dozen cherrystone clams
3 tablespoons oil (preferably olive oil)
1 teaspoon lemon juice
2 cloves garlic, minced
½ teaspoon oregano
⅓ cup minced fresh parsley or chives
1 cup dry whole-wheat *or* rye bread crumbs
¼ cup Parmesan cheese

Now follow these steps:

1. Preheat oven to 425 degrees.
2. Wash clams well, scrubbing off dirt and sand with a stiff brush.
3. Spread clams on a lightly greased cookie sheet. Heat in oven for 1 minute. Check to see if the shells have opened. If they have, remove from the oven. If they have not, heat for another minute or until they do. Let the clams cool until you can handle them.
4. Take off the top shells and throw them away. Place the clams (still in the bottom shells) in a greased, 9″ × 12″ baking pan.
5. Mix all of the remaining ingredients together and sprinkle over the clams.
6. Bake 5 minutes. Serve hot.

TOFU-FISH BALLS

Get these ingredients ready:

½ pound tofu*, drained
½ pound fish fillets (flounder or sole)
1 onion
2 cups dried bread crumbs
1 egg
1½ teaspoons tamari sauce* *or* salt
¼ cup minced scallions

Now follow these steps:

1. Chop the fish, tofu, and onion into ½-inch chunks. Put into blender.
2. Drop the egg, tamari sauce or salt, and 1½ cups of the bread crumbs into the blender on top of the fish, tofu, and onion.
3. Whiz on purée (medium high) until smooth, about 1 minute.
4. Turn into medium-size bowl and mix in the scallions.
5. Form into balls about 1-1½ inches wide. (Makes 18-24.) Roll balls in the remaining ½ cup bread crumbs. Place on a plate or tray, cover with waxed paper or plastic wrap and refrigerate for 2-6 hours.
6. Pour 2 inches of oil into a medium-size pan. Using a deep-fry thermometer, heat the oil to 375 degrees.
7. Carefully drop in 4-5 balls and cook until golden (about 4 minutes). Repeat until all balls are cooked, placing cooked ones on paper towels to drain.
8. Eat plain or dipped in Tamari or Sweet and Sour Sauce.

BAKED TUNA PUFFS

Get these ingredients ready:

1 7-ounce can tuna, well drained
¼ cup mayonnaise *or* Tofu Mayonnaise (page 164)
2 tablespoons chopped pickles or cucumber
2 tablespoons chopped celery
¼ cup minced onion
2 tablespoons sunflower seeds (optional)
1 teaspoon lemon *or* pickle juice
¼ – ½ cup grated cheese (optional)
2 whole-wheat English muffins, split and toasted

Now follow these steps:

1. Preheat oven to 400 degrees.
2. Mix all ingredients except muffins together in a small bowl.
3. Put ¼ of the mixture on each English muffin half.
4. Place on a cookie sheet. Bake 15–20 minutes or until golden and puffy.

Naturally Good Tip: After you have finished using the blender, squirt a drop or two of dishwashing liquid in it. Fill half full with water, cover, and whiz on high for a minute. Almost clean!

TUNA-TOFU LOAF

Get these ingredients ready:

1 7-ounce can tuna, well drained
1 cup crumbled tofu*, well drained
3 eggs, slightly beaten
¼ cup bread crumbs
1 small onion, minced
1 tablespoon chopped parsley *or* chives
½ cup tomato sauce *or* tahini*
½ teaspoon salt
½ teaspoon baking powder
2 teaspoons Italian seasoning *or* tamari sauce*

Now follow these steps:

1. In a medium-size bowl, break up the tuna into flakes. Add remaining ingredients (except tofu) and mix with a fork until well blended.
2. Gently mix in the tofu.
3. Pour into a greased 8" × 4" × 3" loaf pan. Smooth the top with a wet knife. Cover with waxed paper or plastic wrap and put in the refrigerator. Let set for 1 hour to 1 day (not any longer!).
4. Preheat oven to 350 degrees.
5. Bake 50–60 minutes or until browned on top.
6. Remove and serve hot, sliced, with sauce or chill and slice for sandwiches. Good sauce choices are: tomato sauce or mushroom soup thinned with water.

LICKETY-SPLIT LASAGNA

Get these ingredients ready:

8 ounces whole-wheat lasagna
1 quart jar good spaghetti sauce
12 ounces tofu*, crumbled
8 ounces mozzarella cheese, shredded
1 teaspoon salt
1 teaspoon oregano *or* basil
1 teaspoon parsley
¼ cup Parmesan cheese (optional)

Now follow these steps:

1. Preheat oven to 375 degrees.
2. Place a layer of spaghetti sauce (about ½ cup) in a 7" × 11" baking pan. Spread the sauce to cover the bottom of the pan.
3. Layer three pieces of uncooked lasagna over the sauce. (Break in half if too long for the pan.)
4. Mix the tofu, mozzarella cheese, and seasonings together in a small bowl. Spoon about ⅓ of this mixture over the noodles.
5. Repeat these layers (spaghetti sauce, lasagna, tofu mixture) twice more.
6. Sprinkle with Parmesan cheese (if using).
7. Cover pan tightly with aluminum foil; bake 1½ hours. Remove the foil for the last 15 minutes. Let stand 10–15 minutes before serving.

NOT TOO CHEESY MACARONI

Get these ingredients ready:

12 ounces soft tofu*
½ cup soy *or* dairy milk
½ teaspoon dry mustard
½ teaspoon salt
1 teaspoon tamari sauce* (optional)
¼ teaspoon paprika
1 tablespoon margarine
1–2 cups grated Cheddar cheese
½ cup chopped scallions (optional)
8 ounces whole-wheat macaroni, cooked

Now follow these steps:

1. Preheat oven to 350 degrees.
2. Whiz tofu, milk, seasonings and margarine in a blender until smooth, about one minute.
3. Put the cooked and drained macaroni into a medium-large greased casserole.
4. Dump the cheese and scallions (if using) on top. Mix in gently but well.
5. Bake, uncovered, 20–30 minutes.

NUTTY NOODLE CASSEROLE

Get these ingredients ready:

8 ounces whole-wheat noodles
3 large onions, sliced
4 cloves garlic, minced
¼ cup vegetable oil
1 pound fresh spinach, washed
¾ cup chopped almonds
12 ounces tofu*
1 tablespoon tamari sauce*
2 tablespoons vegetable oil
¼ cup crushed corn flakes

Now follow these steps:

1. Cook noodles according to package directions or by using the handy tip on page 111.
2. Preheat oven to 350 degrees.
3. Sauté the onions and garlic in the ¼ cup oil for 10 minutes in a large frying pan. Stir in the almonds and cook 5 minutes.
4. Clean spinach, discarding tough stems, and tear into bite-size pieces. Pile on top of the onion-garlic-almond mixture. Cover the pan and steam for 5 minutes at a low-to-medium temperature.
5. Crumble the tofu into the blender jar *or* a large bowl. Add tamari sauce and blend on high speed *or* cream with an electric mixer until smooth.
6. Grease a large casserole. Make alternate layers of noodles, onion-spinach mixture, and tofu. (You can just mix it all together if you prefer.)
7. Mix the corn flakes and oil together and sprinkle on top.
8. Bake, uncovered, 30 minutes.

STIR-FRIED VEGGIES AND SAUCE

Get these ingredients ready:

Sauce: 2 cloves garlic
2 teaspoons minced fresh ginger
⅓ cup cornstarch *or* arrowroot
1 tablespoon maple syrup (optional)
¼ cup tamari sauce
¼ cup rice *or* apple cider vinegar
½ cup water
1½ cups vegetable broth *or* 2 vegetable bouillon
cubes and 1½ cups water
3 tablespoons oil
1 cup sliced fresh broccoli (flowerets and stems)
1 cup cauliflower flowerets
1 cup sliced carrots
1 cup red cabbage (in 1″ squares)
2 medium onions, sliced

Now follow these steps:

1. Whiz Sauce ingredients in blender until smooth, about 1 minute on high speed. Set aside.
2. Heat oil in a large frying pan or wok. Add broccoli and cauliflower; stir-fry for 1 minute on high heat, stirring constantly.
3. Add carrots and continue to stir-fry for 2 minutes longer.
4. Add cabbage and stir-fry another 2 minutes on medium heat, continuing to stir often.
5. Add onions and cook 1 more minute.
6. Add sauce from blender and cook and stir until thickened, about three minutes. Serve over any grain or pasta. Brown rice and millet are especially good.

GREEN PIES

Get these ingredients ready:

2 pounds raw spinach
3 onions, minced
¼ cup lemon juice
1 cup walnuts
1 cup oil
1 recipe Tofu Pastry (page 142)

Now follow these steps:

1. Wash the spinach, shake dry, and cut into small pieces with scissors or a knife.
2. Put the walnuts in a blender and whiz on high speed until very finely chopped. (You may have to turn the blender on and off to keep the nuts moving.)
3. Mix the spinach, onions, walnuts and oil together in a large bowl until well blended.
4. Make the pastry as instructed in the recipe and cut into 3-inch squares with a pastry cutter or sharp knife. Put 1 heaping tablespoon of filling on each square and fold the top over. With a fork, press around the edges of the pastry to seal. Use a spatula to carefully transfer the little "pies" to cookie sheets, leaving an inch between each one.
5. Preheat oven to 350 degrees. Bake 15–20 minutes. Good warm or cold.

TANGY TOFU-BEAN CASSEROLE

Get these ingredients ready:

2–3 cups frozen tofu*, thawed and drained
2 cups cooked (or 1 20-ounce can) chickpeas, drained
2 cups cooked (or 1 20-ounce can) kidney beans, drained
2 cups cooked corn
1 large onion, chopped
2 cloves garlic, minced
2 tablespoons oil
¼ cup barley malt syrup *or* maple syrup
2 tablespoons prepared mustard
2 umeboshi plums* (pitted and mashed) *or* 3 tablespoons
     apple cider vinegar
½ cup water

Now follow these steps:

1. Preheat oven to 325 degrees.
2. Sauté tofu, onions, and garlic in oil.
3. Dump into a greased dutch oven or large casserole. Mix in all remaining ingredients.
4. Cover with lid or aluminum foil and bake 1 hour. Good served over millet.

CORNY BEANCAKES

Get these ingredients ready:

2 cups cornmeal
½ teaspoon salt
1 cup cooked pinto *or* kidney beans
1 tablespoon miso*
2 cups boiling water
¼ cup oil

Now follow these steps:

1. Mix the cornmeal and salt in a medium-size pan.
2. Slowly stir in the boiling water, being careful not to let it get lumpy. Cook, over low heat until thick, about 5–10 minutes.
3. Put a piece of waxed paper on the counter and drop 8 equal-sized portions of cornmeal on it. Let stand until cool enough to handle.
4. Divide each portion into 2 and form each into a 2-inch round cake with your hands. You will have 16 little cakes.
5. Put the beans and miso into a small bowl and mash together until fairly smooth (there will still be little lumps).
6. Put 2 tablespoons of the bean mixture on 8 of the cornmeal cakes. Top with the remaining 8 cornmeal cakes and press around the edges with a fork (like pastry) to seal.
7. Put the ¼ cup oil in a large frying pan on medium high heat. When hot (about 30 seconds), put the filled cornmeal cakes in and fry until golden brown. Turn and brown the other side, adding a bit more oil if you need it. Pretty sprinkled with chopped scallions.

SUPER SANDWICHES

Tofu Egg Salad

> 1 hardboiled egg, chopped
> ¼ cup tofu*, crumbled
> ¼ cup mayonnaise *or* Tofu Mayonnaise(page 164)
> 2 tablespoons minced celery
> 1 tablespoon minced chives or onion

Mix ingredients together with fork and pile on whole-grain bread or toast. Top with lettuce or greens. Serves 1.

Tuna-Apple Salad

> 1 7-ounce can tuna, drained
> 1 small apple, unpeeled and grated
> 2 tablespoons Tofu Mayonnaise(page 164)*or* ¼ cup tofu*
> ¼ tablespoon salt
> 1–2 tablespoons minced onion *or* scallions

Break up the tuna in a small bowl. Mix in remaining ingredients, mashing the tofu, if using it. Good on whole-grain, raisin, or pita bread. Serves 2 or 3.

Leftover Fillet Spread

> 1 cup leftover, cooked fillet of fish
> ¼ cup mayonnaise or Tofu Mayonnaise (page 164)
> 2 tablespoons minced celery or cucumber
> 2 tablespoons shredded carrot
> pinch of salt
> 1 teaspoon lemon juice (optional)

Mix all ingredients together in a small bowl. Spread on bread or toast (oatmeal bread is good). Serves 2.

Peanut Butter Plus

¼ cup natural peanut butter
2 tablespoons tahini*
1–2 tablespoons currants or raisins

Mix everything together in a small bowl and spread on whole-wheat pita bread. Tasty with sprouts on top. Serves 1.

Baked Bean Sandwich

½ cup leftover baked beans
1 slice mild onion
1 tablespoon sugar-free catsup

Spread the beans on a thick slice of bread (sourdough rye is good) and mash a bit with a fork. Separate the onion slice into rings and arrange on top of the beans. Spread with the catsup, cover with another slice of bread, and eat. Serves 1.

SLOPPY SOYJOY

Get these ingredients ready:

1 pound (2 8-ounce packages) tempeh*
1 large onion, chopped
1 small green pepper, minced
2 tablespoons oil
1 tablespoon tamari sauce*
2 tablespoons barley malt syrup*
2 tablespoons apple cider vinegar
1 cup spaghetti sauce

Now follow these steps:

1. Cut tempeh into ½-inch cubes.
2. Sauté tempeh, onions, and green pepper in the oil for 5 minutes.
3. Stir in the remaining ingredients and simmer for 20 minutes.
4. Serve on whole-grain rolls (cut in half) or over wide noodles. Great with corn-on-the-cob and cucumber salad.

Side Shows

Ladies and gentlemen:

Let me introduce you to a cast of hundreds! The supporting roles are played by vegetables, beans, pasta, and grains.

You and your friends might like to get together for a "potluck" supper. If each of you fixes one "side show," together you'll have a three-ring "main event."

If dinner seems too long to wait...how about lunch? Any of these "side show" dishes can be balanced with carrot sticks, pickles, and whole-grain bread or crackers for a tasty meal.

In fact, breakfast, lunch, dinner, snacktime, *anytime* is the right time for these whole foods.

CAULIFLOWER AND ZUCCHINI CRUNCH

Get these ingredients ready:

1 small head cauliflower
3 medium zucchini, unpeeled
1 large onion
2 cloves garlic, minced
3 eggs, well-beaten
1 cup whole-wheat flour
1 tablespoon tamari sauce*
1 teaspoon rosemary
⅓ cup oil
½ cup Parmesan cheese (optional)

Now follow these steps:

1. Preheat oven to 375 degrees.
2. Grate or chop the cauliflower, zucchini, and onion. Combine with garlic and eggs in a large bowl. Mix in remaining ingredients and stir well.
3. Pour into a greased 9″ × 13″ pan.
4. Bake 1 hour. Let stand for 20 minutes before cutting into squares and serving.

SUNNY BEETS

Get these ingredients ready:

1 bunch beets, well scrubbed
1 cup fresh orange juice
2 tablespoons arrowroot
1 tablespoon maple syrup *or* honey
2 tablespoons oil
1 tablespoon lemon juice

Now follow these steps:

1. Cut the tops off about an inch above the beets. Put in a saucepan, cover with water, and bring to a boil over high heat. Lower the heat and cook, covered, for 30–40 minutes. Pour off the water and let beets cool. Remove the skins, cut off the tops, and slice the beets about ½-inch thick.
2. In a small bowl, slowly stir the orange juice into the arrowroot. Add the maple syrup *or* honey.
3. Heat the oil in a medium-size saucepan over medium heat. Slowly stir the orange juice mixture into the oil. Cook, stirring constantly, until clear and thickened. Remove from heat and stir in the lemon juice. Pour over the beet slices and serve.

BAKED CARROTS

Get these ingredients ready:

 1 pound carrots, pared or well scrubbed
 ½ teaspoon salt
 1 teaspoon maple syrup
 2 tablespoons margarine

Now follow these steps:

1. Preheat oven to 325 degrees.
2. Cut carrots in halves or thirds, depending on size. Place in 1-quart casserole.
3. Sprinkle with salt and maple syrup; dot with margarine. Cover casserole.
4. Bake 1 hour 15 minutes. (If you prefer to bake at 350 degrees, bake for 1 hour only.)

NOT REALLY RATATOUILLE

Get these ingredients ready:

1 pound green beans, snapped in half
3 onions, chopped
3 cloves garlic, minced
2 green peppers, chopped (seeds removed!)
½ cup oil, preferably olive oil
3 medium zucchini
4 tomatoes, peeled and chopped
2 teaspoons Italian seasoning *or* 1 teaspoon each oregano
   and basil
¼ cup chopped fresh parsley *or* 2 tablespoons dried parsley
1 teaspoon salt

Now follow these steps:

1. In a large frying pan or dutch oven, sauté the onions, garlic, and green pepper in the oil for 10 minutes on medium heat, stirring occasionally.
2. Cut the zucchini in quarters lengthwise, then slice in 1-inch chunks. (Take out the seeds if there are too many for your taste.)
3. Pile the zucchini and all of the remaining ingredients on top of the onion-garlic-pepper mixture. Mix together gently, cover, and simmer for 30 minutes on low heat.
4. Remove the cover, raise heat and boil for 5 to 10 minutes or until the liquid is reduced to your liking.
5. Serve as a side dish or over brown rice as a main dish. Tasty with sesame seeds sprinkled on top.

Naturally Good Tip: Want to keep that fresh parsley (or other herb) crisp and green? Find a jar large enough to hold it and put about ½-inch of water in the bottom. Now put in the herb, stems down, screw on the top, and refrigerate. Keeps fresh for about a week.

GREAT GREENS

Get these ingredients ready:

1 bunch kale *or* other greens
2 onions, chopped
2 cloves garlic, minced
2 small carrots *or* white turnips, diced
2 tablespoons oil, preferably sesame
1 tablespoon rice vinegar or lemon juice

Now follow these steps:

1. Wash greens well and trim off tough stems. Mix with remaining ingredients in a large saucepan or wok.
2. Cover and steam over medium heat for 15–20 minutes.

ITALIAN BEANS

Get these ingredients ready:

1 onion, chopped
4 cloves garlic, minced
6 tablespoons oil
2 cups (or 1 15-ounce can) cooked kidney beans, drained
2 cups (or 1 15-ounce can) cooked chickpeas, drained
1 teaspoon basil
1 teaspoon oregano
2 tomatoes, peeled and chopped (optional)
3 cups zucchini *or* cauliflower , chopped

Now follow these steps:

1. Preheat oven to 375 degrees.
2. Sauté the onion and garlic in the oil for 5 minutes.
3. Mix with remaining ingredients in a large greased casserole or dutch oven.
4. Cover and bake 30 minutes.

BAKED BEAN CASSEROLE

Get these ingredients ready:

1 large green pepper, diced
2 medium onions, chopped
½ pound mushrooms, chopped
2 tablespoons oil
3 1-pound cans Vegetarian Beans
¾ cup catsup
⅓ cup prepared mustard
1 cup maple syrup
1½ teaspoons oregano
5 whole cloves
3 bay leaves

Now follow these steps:

1. In a large saucepan or frying pan, sauté pepper, onions, and mushrooms in oil until just tender.
2. Add remaining ingredients and heat on top of stove just long enough to blend flavors. Serve immediately *or* store in refrigerator and reheat later by baking for 30 minutes in a 400 degree oven.

ALL DAY LONG BEAN BAKE

Get these ingredients ready:

1 cup navy beans
1 cup kidney beans
2 onions, sliced
3 cloves garlic, minced
1 cup sliced mushrooms
4 cups sliced carrots
¼ cup oil
½ cup barley
1 cup water
1 pound green beans, snapped in half
1 teaspoon basil
½ teaspoon oregano
1 bay leaf

Now follow these steps:

1. Soak beans overnight as directed in "How to Cook Beans" (page 53). Drain and place in large casserole or dutch oven.
2. Sauté onions, garlic, mushrooms, and carrots in oil.
3. Mix sautéed vegetables with beans and remaining ingredients. Pour more hot water over until ingredients are covered by ½-inch of water.
4. Cover. Place in oven and set temperature at 225 degrees (no need to preheat). Cook all day long (8–12 hours).

EASY BEANS AND BARLEY

Get these ingredients ready:

2 tablespoons oil
1 onion, chopped
2 cloves garlic, minced
2 tomatoes, peeled and chopped *or* 1 8-ounce can stewed
  tomatoes
1 medium zucchini, chopped
½ teaspoon salt
½ teaspoon thyme
1 16-ounce can beans (your choice)
3 cups cooked barley *or* any cooked grain

Now follow these steps:

1. Heat the oil in a large frying pan and sauté the onion and garlic for 5 minutes over medium heat, stirring once in a while.
2. Add the tomatoes, zucchini, salt, and thyme. Cover pan, lower heat, and simmer about 15 minutes.
3. Stir in beans and heat through. If using leftover cold barley or grain, mix in and heat through. If using freshly cooked, warm barley or grain, just spoon your cooked mixture over it.

Naturally Good Tip: Wet the top edge of your pan and the bottom edge of the lid when cooking grains. It will make a tight seal and the grain will steam better. Never remove the lid and stir before the grains are done!

BAKED BULGUR

Get these ingredients ready:

¼ cup oil, preferably sesame oil
1 onion, minced
3 cloves garlic, minced
¼ cup sesame seeds
2 cups uncooked bulgur
½ cup chopped fresh herb *or* 1 tablespoon dried herb of
    your choice (such as parsley, chives, dill, or marjoram)
4 cups Vegetable Broth (page 115) *or* 4 cups water and 4
    vegetable bouillon cubes

Now follow these steps:

1. Preheat oven to 350 degrees.
2. Sauté the onion, garlic, and sesame seeds in the oil for 5
   minutes.
3. Add the bulgur to the sautéed vegetables and cook for 5
   minutes longer, stirring often.
4. Mix in the herb and the vegetable broth *or* water and bouillon
   cubes. (Mash the cubes with a fork to break them up.)
5. Pour into a large, greased casserole and bake, covered, for
   45 minutes.
6. Remove from oven, and stir with a fork to fluff up. Good
   with Baked Carrots (page 103) and Cole Slaw (page 117) or a
   tossed green salad.

MIXED GRAIN LOAF

Get these ingredients ready:

4 cups mixed cooked grains (leftover rice, millet, and barley are good)
4 cups grated carrots
1 cup almond butter
1 cup fresh whole-wheat bread crumbs
1 onion, minced
2 tablespoons oil
1 teaspoon dill
1 teaspoon basil
1 teaspoon salt

Now follow these steps:

1. Preheat oven to 350 degrees.
2. In a small frying pan, sauté the onion in the oil for 5 minutes.
3. Mix the onions and all the remaining ingredients together
   in a large mixing bowl, using a wooden spoon or clean hands.
4. Grease a 9″ × 5″ × 3″ bread pan. Dump the grain mixture
   into the pan and smooth the top.
5. Bake 45–50 minutes. Take from the oven and let stand a
   few minutes before turning out onto a plate and slicing.

NOODLES ROMANOFF

Get these ingredients ready:

1 pound whole-wheat *or* spinach noodles
1 cup crumbled tofu*
1 cup soy *or* dairy yogurt
1 cup grated Parmesan cheese (optional)
¼ cup minced onion
1 clove garlic, minced
½ teaspoon salt
1 teaspoon tamari sauce*
¼ cup crushed corn flakes *or* bread crumbs
2 tablespoons oil

Now follow these steps:

1. Cook the noodles as directed on the package or according to the tip on the bottom of this page. Drain well.
2. Preheat oven to 350 degrees.
3. Combine the remaining ingredients, *except the oil and crumbs,* in a large bowl. Dump the noodles on top and mix all together with a wooden spoon.
4. Pour into a large, well greased casserole.
5. Mix the oil and crumbs together in a small bowl. Sprinkle on top of the noodle mixture.
6. Bake, uncovered, 45 minutes. Eat while hot.

Naturally Good Tip: To cook noodles easily without having to watch the pot, just bring the amount of water recommended on the package directions to a full boil. Slowly drop in the noodles so that boiling does not stop. Stir and cover the pan tightly. Remove from heat. Let stand for 20 minutes. Drain.

ANOTHER NOODLE BAKE

Get these ingredients ready:

½-pound wide noodles
2 cups frozen tofu*, thawed
2 tablespoons oil
1 8-ounce can tomato sauce
1 teaspoon salt
½ teaspoon basil *or* oregano
1 cup yogurt *or* crumbled tofu*
⅔ cup chopped scallions
½ cup Cheddar cheese (optional)

Now follow these steps:

1. Cook the noodles as directed on the package or according to the tip on page 111. Drain well.
2. Preheat oven to 350 degrees.
3. Cut the thawed tofu into cubes and sauté in the oil for 5 minutes.
4. Mix in the tomato sauce, ½ teaspoon of the salt, and basil or oregano. Simmer for 5 minutes longer.
5. Combine the yogurt *or* crumbled tofu, remaining ½ teaspoon salt, and scallions in a large bowl. Fold in the noodles.
6. Put half of the noodle mix in a large, greased casserole. Cover with half of the sautéed tofu mixture. Repeat once again.
7. Sprinkle with the cheese, if using.
8. Bake, uncovered, 25 minutes.

Naturally Good Tip: If your pasta is always getting stuck together, try adding 1 tablespoon of oil to the cooking water the next time. By the way, pasta is good cooked without the salt.

BAKED VEGETABLE SOUP

Get these ingredients ready:

3 tablespoons oil
2 carrots, sliced
3 onions *or* 1 bunch leeks, sliced
1 small white turnip, minced
2 celery stalks, thinly sliced
1 cup green beans, cut in ½-inch pieces
1 cup cauliflower flowerets
1 bay leaf
1 teaspoon salt
1 teaspoon dillweed
4 cups water
2 vegetable bouillon cubes

Now follow these steps:

1. Preheat oven to 300 degrees.
2. Heat the oil in a dutch oven or large ovenproof casserole over medium heat.
3. Dump all the vegetables in and sauté for about 15 minutes, stirring every few minutes.
4. Add remaining ingredients, stir, and bring to a boil.
5. Cover and put in oven. Bake 1½ hours.

JAN'S SQUASH SOUP

Get these ingredients ready:

1 medium butternut squash *or* 2 acorn squash
1 medium onion, chopped
1 tablespoon oil
½ teaspoon basil
1 vegetable bouillon cube
Water *or* milk

Now follow these steps:

1. Peel squash, remove seeds, and cut into chunks. Place in large saucepan, cover with water and cook until very soft (about 20–30 minutes). Don't drain.
2. While squash is cooking, sauté the onion in the oil until it just begins to brown.
3. Put the squash in a blender with the bouillon cube and enough of the cooking water to blend easily. Blend until smooth and dump it back into the pan. Mix in the onions and enough water or milk to make it as thick or as thin as you like. Stir in basil and heat.

VEGETABLE BROTH

Get these ingredients ready:

8 cups (2 quarts) water
2 large onions
2 large stalks celery
2 large carrots
2 leeks (optional)
1 medium turnip (optional)
1 cup green beans (optional)
1 cup lettuce (optional)
5 cloves garlic
1 bay leaf
¼ cup fresh or 2 tablespoons dried parsley
1 tablespoon tamari* sauce
1 teaspoon salt

Now follow these steps:

1. Cut up all the vegetables into large chunks. (Clean, but don't peel any except for the garlic.) Place in large saucepan with the water.
2. Add remaining ingredients. Cover. Bring to boil over high heat, then turn to low and simmer for at least 1 hour (2 to 3 hours would be even better).
3. Strain through a colander placed over a large bowl or pan. Use immediately or refrigerate for up to 1 week or freeze for up to 3 months.

GREEN SALAD SPECIAL

Get these ingredients ready:

6 cups clean greens (lettuce, spinach, chicory, endive, etc.)
1–2 cups chopped or sliced vegetables (cucumber, carrots, cauliflower, mushrooms, zucchini, etc.)
½ cup sunflower seeds or chopped nuts
½ cup beansprouts (optional)
¼ cup chopped scallions or onions

Now follow these steps:

1. Mix everything together in a large salad bowl. Toss gently with 2–4 tablespoons of your favorite salad dressing.
2. Experiment! Add leftovers or anything that looks good from the fridge!

CUKE SALAD

Get these ingredients ready:

3 cucumbers
⅓ cup mild vinegar
1 tablespoon apple juice concentrate
1 teaspoon tamari sauce

Now follow these steps:

1. Peel the cucumbers if they have been waxed. Slice into thin rounds.
2. Mix together the remaining ingredients in a small bowl. Pour over the cucumbers in a medium-size bowl.
3. Let stand, covered, in the refrigerator for at least 1 hour before eating. Stays fresh for about 5 days.

COLE SLAW

Get these ingredients ready:

2 cups shredded green or red cabbage
1 carrot, shredded
1 small cucumber, shredded
1 small onion, shredded
3 tablespoons maple syrup
3 tablespoons apple cider vinegar
1 tablespoon water
2 tablespoons oil
2 teaspoons salt

Now follow these steps:

1. Mix shredded vegetables together in a medium-size mixing or serving bowl.
2. Combine remaining ingredients and pour over vegetables. Mix well.
3. Let stand in refrigerator for at least 3 hours before serving.

WALDORF SALAD

Get these ingredients ready:

6 apples
1 teaspoon lemon juice
½ cup minced celery
½ cup chopped nuts
⅓ cup mayonnaise *or* tofu mayonnaise (page 164)

Now follow these steps:

1. Wash and dry apples but don't peel them. Core and cut into ½-inch cubes.
2. Mix in the lemon juice to keep the apples from turning brown.
3. Stir in the remaining ingredients. Refrigerate for at least ½ hour before eating.

SUMMER SALAD MOLD

Get these ingredients ready:

2 heaping tablespoons agar* flakes
1½ cups orange juice *or* apple juice
2 tablespoons maple syrup (optional)
2 cups sliced strawberries
1 banana, thinly sliced
½–1 cup chopped walnuts, raw or toasted

Now follow these steps:

1. Sprinkle the agar on 3 tablespoons of the juice in a small bowl.
2. Put the remaining juice in a small saucepan and bring to a boil. Add the agar-juice and continue to boil and stir for 1 minute. Remove from heat.
3. Fold in the remaining ingredients. Pour into large mold or bowl and chill until firm.

HOLIDAY SALAD MOLD

Get these ingredients ready:

2½ tablespoons agar* flakes
1 cup apple juice
¼ cup maple syrup
1 cup chopped raw cranberries
½ cup chopped nuts, preferably roasted

Now follow these steps:

1. Sprinkle the agar on 2 tablespoons of the apple juice in a small bowl.
2. Put the remaining apple juice and maple syrup in a small saucepan and bring to a boil. Stir in the agar-juice and boil for 1 minute, stirring often.
3. Stir in the remaining ingredients. Pour into a 3–4 cup mold and chill until firm.

CARROT-PINEAPPLE MOLD

Get these ingredients ready:

2 heaping tablespoons agar* flakes
1½ cups apple juice *or* cider *or* orange juice
1½ cups grated carrots
1 8-ounce can crushed pineapple
1 tablespoon lemon juice
Pinch of salt

Now follow these steps:

1. Sprinkle the agar on 3 tablespoons of the juice in a small bowl.
2. Put the remaining juice in a small saucepan and bring to a boil. Add the agar-juice and continue to boil and stir for 1 minute. Remove from heat.
3. Add the remaining ingredients. Pour into 1-quart mold or bowl and chill until firm.

> **Naturally Good Tip:** To unmold gelatin (or agar) mold easily, get out a flat plate that is larger than the mold. Wipe the plate with a damp towel and place the filled mold, upside down on the plate. Now, run hot water over a small towel and wring out most of the water so that the towel is just damp but still hot. Quickly and carefully (it's hot!) wrap the towel around the top and sides of the mold. Let stand while you count to 30. Remove the towel and slip off the mold. (You can make it even easier by very lightly oiling the mold before you pour in the gelatin mixture.)

APPLESAUCE BROWN BREAD

Get these ingredients ready:

2 cups whole-wheat flour
1 cup cornmeal
½ teaspoon salt
1 teaspoon baking soda
1 cup water
1 cup barley malt *or* ¾ cup maple syrup
¾ cup unsweetened applesauce
¾ cup raisins

Now follow these steps:

1. Preheat oven to 350 degrees.
2. Combine dry ingredients in large mixing bowl.
3. Add water and barley malt *or* maple syrup. Mix with a wooden spoon until smooth.
4. Fold in applesauce and raisins.
5. Pour into a greased 9-inch square pan and bake 35 minutes. Cut into squares to serve. Good with baked beans and cole slaw.

CRANAPPLE QUICK BREAD

Get these ingredients ready:

2 tablespoons margarine
2 tablespoons oil
¾ cup maple syrup *or* ½ cup maple syrup and ¼ cup honey
1 egg
1 cup cranberry-apple juice
2 teaspoons baking powder
1 cup fresh cranberries, cut in half
2¼ cups whole wheat flour
½ cup chopped walnuts

Now follow these steps:

1. Preheat oven to 350 degrees.
2. Beat margarine, oil, maple syrup (and honey, if used) and egg together with an electric mixer for 1½ minutes, in a medium-size bowl.
3. Slowly beat in cranberry-apple juice until smooth, about another ½ minute.
4. Combine dry ingredients in a small bowl. Add to first mixture all at once. Stir with wooden spoon just until smooth. Fold in cranberries and nuts.
5. Pour into greased 9" × 5" × 3" bread pan. Bake 60–70 minutes. Let cool in pan on rack 10–15 minutes. Turn out on rack to finish cooling. Wrap in foil to store.

SUNFLOWER BREAD

Get these ingredients ready:

2 tablespoons margarine
1 cup maple syrup *or* rice syrup
1 egg
¾ cup orange juice (preferably fresh)
2 tablespoons grated orange rind
1 tablespoon baking powder
½ teaspoon salt
2 cups whole-wheat flour
1 cup sunflower seeds, raw or toasted

Now follow these steps:

1. Preheat oven to 325 degrees.
2. Beat margarine, maple syrup *or* rice syrup, and egg with electric mixer for 1 minute in a medium size bowl.
3. Combine remaining ingredients together in a small bowl. Add to first mixture, all at once. Mix well with a wooden spoon just until smooth.
4. Pour into greased 9″ × 5″ × 3″ bread pan. Bake for 1 hour. Let cool in pan on rack 10–15 minutes. Turn out on rack to finish cooling. Wrap in foil to store.

WONDERFUL WHEATBERRY BREAD

Get these ingredients ready:

¾ cup whole-wheat berries
2 cups water
1 cup whole-wheat flour
1 cup chopped nuts
1 teaspoon baking soda
1 teaspoon salt
½ cup crumbled tofu*
½ cup water
¼ cup barley malt or maple syrup
2 tablespoons oil

Now follow these steps:

1. Combine whole-wheat berries and water in medium-size saucepan. Bring to boil over medium heat and boil for 2 minutes. Turn off heat, cover saucepan, and let stand for 1 to 2 hours. Bring to boil again and simmer, uncovered, 1½ hours or until tender.
2. Preheat oven to 350 degrees.
3. Mix flour, nuts, baking soda, and salt in a large bowl.
4. Place tofu, water, barley malt or maple syrup, and oil in blender and blend until smooth.
5. Stir tofu mixture into flour mixture and mix just until dry ingredients are all moistened. Drain whole-wheat berries and fold into bread mixture. Pour into greased 8" × 4" bread pan.
6. Bake 1 hour. Let cool in pan for 10 minutes, then turn out on wire rack to finish cooling.

Finales

Are you at the desserts *already?*

This is a cookbook so, naturally, there are a lot of devastatingly delicious recipes here but try to remember that an apple is the best dessert of all! (Of course, Apple Cookies are good...and Apple Butter Bread...and Apple Cake...and Apple Granola Crisp...and Apple Noodle Dessert...)

CRANAPPLE PEAR CRISP

Get these ingredients ready:

2 cups pared, sliced pears
2 cups pared, sliced apples
1 pound fresh cranberries
1¼ cups whole-wheat flour
1 teaspoon cinnamon *or* vanilla
1 cup maple syrup
¼ cup honey
½ cup margarine *or* ⅓ cup oil

Now follow these steps:

1. Preheat oven to 350 degrees.
2. Grease a 9″×13″ baking dish with 1 tablespoon oil or margarine.
3. Put the apples, pears, and cranberries in the baking dish.
4. Mix the whole-wheat flour, maple syrup, honey, cinnamon *or* vanilla, and margarine *or* oil in a medium mixing bowl with your hands just until the mixture is lumpy. Sprinkle over the fruit mixture.
5. Bake 50–60 minutes or until golden. Eat warm or cold.

APPLE GRANOLA CRISP

Get these ingredients ready:

5–6 cups pared, sliced apples
½ cup maple syrup
1 tablespoon lemon juice
2 tablespoons whole-wheat flour
1 cup Honey Almond Granola (page 65)
1½ teaspoons apple pie spice
¼ cup margarine *or* oil

Now follow these steps:

1. Preheat oven to 375 degrees.
2. Mix apples with 3 tablespoons of the maple syrup and the lemon juice. Dump into a greased casserole or an 8-inch square pan.
3. Mix remaining ingredients until crumbly. Spread over apples.
4. Bake 40 minutes. Serve warm or at room temperature.

SWEET 'N' SPICY APPLE NOODLE DESSERT

Get these ingredients ready:

6 ounces whole-wheat noodles
¼ cup sesame oil
3 cups homemade *or* unsweetened applesauce
2 eggs
½ cup honey
2 teaspoons vanilla
¼ teaspoon almond extract
1 teaspoon cinnamon
1 cup raisins
½ cup chopped almonds, preferably toasted

Now follow these steps:

1. Cook the noodles as directed on the package or according to the tip on page 111. Drain well.
2. Preheat oven to 375 degrees.
3. Mix the noodles with the oil. Add all the other ingredients and mix again.
4. Pour into a greased 8-inch square pan.
5. Bake 45 minutes. Cut in squares to serve. Good warm or cool.

BANANA RAISIN BARS

Get these ingredients ready:

½ cup margarine, at room temperature
½ cup maple syrup
2 tablespoons barley malt *or* molasses
1 teaspoon vanilla
1 cup well mashed ripe banana
1½ cups whole-wheat flour *or* ¾ cup each of whole-wheat
  and rye flours
½ teaspoon baking soda
¼ teaspoon salt
1 cup raisins
½–1 cup chopped walnuts *or* almonds

Now follow these steps:

1. Preheat oven to 350 degrees.
2. Cream the margarine, maple syrup, barley malt *or* molasses, and vanilla together with a wooden spoon or electric mixer until creamy, about 2 minutes.
3. Stir in the bananas and mix well.
4. Mix in the flour, baking soda, and salt.
5. Fold in the raisins and half of the nuts.
6. Turn into a lightly greased 9″ × 13″ baking pan. Smooth top. Sprinkle remaining half of the nuts evenly over the top.
7. Bake 20–25 minutes. Remove from oven and let cool on wire rack until cool to the touch before cutting into squares.

Naturally Good Tip: Dropped an egg on the floor? Don't panic! Simply dump some salt on top of the egg mess and let stand while you try to find another egg. Now sweep it all up and throw away the evidence!

HONEY FLAKE MACAROONS

Get these ingredients ready:

4 egg whites, at room temperature
½ cup honey
Pinch of salt
3 cups Corn *or* Barley Nutri-Grain Flaked Cereal
1 cup chopped almonds *or* walnuts
1 cup unsweetened flaked coconut

Now follow these steps:

1. Preheat oven to 300 degrees.
2. Put the egg whites in a large mixing bowl. (Make sure the bowl is very clean and not made of plastic—egg whites won't beat well in plastic.) With an electric mixer on high speed, beat the egg whites until they get foamy. Now add the honey 1 tablespoon at a time until you have used it all. Keep on beating until you have a very stiff mixture. Turn off the mixer. When you lift the beaters from the bowl, the mixture should stand up in peaks.
3. Gently fold in the cereal flakes, nuts, and coconut, using a wooden spoon or spatula.
4. Drop the mixture by tablespoonfuls onto lightly greased cookie sheets. (You should have about 3 dozen cookies.)
5. Bake 20 minutes.
6. Remove from cookie sheets with a spatula and place on wire racks until cool. After cooling, keep well wrapped or covered to keep cookies from getting soggy.

BRAZIL NUT BALLS

Get these ingredients ready:

⅔ cup whole-wheat flour
½ cup maple syrup
½ cup margarine, softened
1 tablespoon grated lemon rind (optional)
1 cup Brazil nuts

Now follow these steps:

1. Put Brazil nuts in the blender and whirl at high speed until they are very finely chopped (like meal). Dump into a medium-size bowl.
2. Mix in the remaining ingredients with an electric mixer or a wooden spoon until smooth. Chill in the refrigerator for 1 hour.
3. Preheat oven to 350 degrees.
4. Form the dough into 1-inch balls and place on ungreased cookie sheets.
5. Bake 10 minutes. Let cool on cookie sheets for 5 minutes before removing to wire racks to finish cooling.

BUTTERSCOTCH BROWNIES

Get these ingredients ready:

½ cup margarine *or* ⅓ cup oil
1 cup maple syrup *or* ¾ cup honey
2 eggs
1 cup whole-wheat flour
¾ cup chopped nuts
1 teaspoon vanilla

Now follow these steps:

1. Preheat oven to 350 degrees.
2. Beat the margarine *or* oil and maple syrup *or* honey in a medium-size mixing bowl until creamy, using an electric mixer or a wooden spoon.
3. Beat in the eggs until well blended.
4. Stir in the flour, nuts, and vanilla until no dry spots remain.
5. Spoon into greased 9-inch square pan.
6. Bake 30 minutes. Cool on wire rack. Cut into squares.

APPLE OF YOUR EYE COOKIES

Get these ingredients ready:

2½ cups wholewheat flour
1 cup oatmeal *or* rolled rye
½ cup raisins
½ cup chopped, unpeeled apples
½ cup chopped nuts
½ teaspoon salt
½ teaspoon cinnamon
½ teaspoon allspice
1 cup apple juice
½ cup maple syrup
½ cup water
1 teaspoon vanilla

Now follow these steps:

1. Preheat oven to 350 degrees.
2. Mix dry ingredients together in a large bowl.
3. Combine the remaining ingredients and dump into the dry ingredients all at once; mix well with a wooden spoon.
4. Let stand for 10 or 15 minutes.
5. Drop by heaping teaspoonfuls onto greased cookie sheets.
6. Bake for 20–25 minutes. Remove with spatula and let cool on wire racks.

CRUNCH COOKIES

Get these ingredients ready:

¼ cup margarine
¾ cup maple syrup *or* ½ cup honey
1 egg
1 tablespoon grated lemon rind
1 teaspoon vanilla
1 cup whole-wheat flour
½ teaspoon salt
½ teaspoon baking powder
1 teaspoon cinnamon
¼ teaspoon ginger
2½ cups Nutri-Grain Corn Flakes crushed to measure
    1¼ cups
½ cup chopped nuts *or* raisins (optional)

Now follow these steps:

1. Preheat oven to 375 degrees.
2. Beat margarine, maple syrup *or* honey, egg, lemon rind, and vanilla together with wood spoon or electric mixer until smooth.
3. Stir in the flour, salt, baking soda, cinnamon, and ginger until smooth.
4. Fold in the crushed corn flakes and nuts *or* raisins (if used) until thoroughly blended.
5. Drop by tablespoonfuls onto ungreased cookie sheets. (You should have about 3 dozen.)
6. Bake about 10 minutes. Remove from cookie sheets with spatula and cool on wire racks.

GINGERBREAD PEOPLE

Get these ingredients ready:

½ cup oil
¼ cup boiling water
½ cup maple syrup
½ cup barley malt syrup *or* molasses
3 cups whole-wheat flour
1 teaspoon baking soda
½ teaspoon salt
1½ teaspoons ginger
½ teaspoon cinnamon
½ teaspoon nutmeg

Now follow these steps:

1. Put oil, water, maple syrup and barley malt *or* molasses in a large bowl and beat until well blended (about 1 minute) with a wooden spoon or electric mixer.
2. Dump in all remaining ingredients and mix until you have a smooth dough.
3. Form the dough into a ball and wrap in waxed paper or plastic wrap. Put in the refrigerator to chill for 1 to 3 hours.
4. Preheat oven to 375 degrees.
5. Remove dough from refrigerator and cut in half. Using a well floured board or pastry cloth and rolling pin, roll each half out ⅛–¼-inch thick. Using cookie cutters, cut out gingerbread people or other shapes. (If you don't have cookie cutters, cut shapes out of cardboard, place on dough and cut around them with a sharp knife. Remove cardboard.) With spatula, place cookies on greased cookie sheets leaving space between them to spread out.
6. Bake 10 minutes. Cool on wire racks and decorate as desired.

APPLE CRUMB BARS

Get these ingredients ready:

2 cups flour
½ teaspoon salt
⅓ cup oil
¾ cup hot water
5–6 sliced apples
1 cup coconut
½ cup Yinnies brand Rice Syrup
¼ teaspoon salt
½ teaspoon cinnamon
2 tablespoons flour
2 tablespoons oil
2 teaspoons vanilla
1 teaspoon grated orange rind
1 egg (optional)

Now follow these steps:

1. Preheat oven to 375 degrees.
2. In a mixing bowl combine the oil, water and salt for the dough.
3. Beat the oil and water together, then add the flour and make a dough. Roll into a rectangle and place on an oiled cookie sheet.
4. Place the sliced apples on the dough in rows.
5. In a bowl combine coconut, Yinnies brand Rice Syrup, oil, salt and spices (and egg, if used). Mix. Sprinkle this mixture over the apples.
6. Bake for 30 minutes. Cool and cut into bars.

Naturally Good Tip: This recipe is reprinted by permission of the people at Chico-San who make Yinnies brand Rice Syrup. If you would like their free 19-page recipe booklet filled with super dessert recipes, send a postcard to: Free Yinnies Cookbook, Chico-San, P.O. Box 1004, Chico, CA 95927. Be sure to include your complete address and ZIP.

SARAH'S STRAWBERRY CAKE

Get these ingredients ready:

1 cup mild oil
3 cups crushed strawberries
1 cup minced dried apricots
1 cup unsweetened shredded coconut
1 cup chopped walnuts
2 cups rolled rye *or* oats
1 teaspoon vanilla
½ teaspoon salt
2 cups whole-wheat flour

Now follow these steps:

1. Preheat oven to 350 degrees.
2. Put all ingredients in a large mixing bowl and mix well with a wooden spoon.
3. Grease and flour 2 9-inch cake pans. Pour batter into pans.
4. Bake 45 minutes.
5. Let cool in pans on wire rack for 10 minutes. Turn out of pans and finish cooling on racks. Frost with Tofu Whip (page 146) or unsweetened whipped cream.

MAPLE NUT SPONGE CAKE

Get these ingredients ready:

4 eggs
¼ teaspoon salt
¾ cup maple syrup
⅔ cup whole-wheat flour
¼ teaspoon almond extract
½ teaspoon baking powder

Now follow these steps:

1. Preheat oven to 325 degrees.
2. Carefully separate egg yolks from egg whites, placing egg whites in a large non-plastic bowl and egg yolks in a medium-size bowl.
3. Beat the egg whites and salt with an electric mixer on high speed until they form stiff peaks. Set aside.
4. Put the maple syrup in a small saucepan and bring it to a boil.
5. When the maple syrup is boiling, slowly pour it into the egg whites, beating with the electric mixer at high speed all the while. (Just drizzle the syrup in. If you pour too quickly, you will cook the egg whites and they will be stringy!)
6. Without washing the mixer beaters, beat the egg yolks for 1 minute. Beat in the almond extract until well blended.
7. Fold the egg yolk mixture into the egg white mixture. Now gently fold in the almonds and baking powder, just until evenly distributed. Don't over mix.
8. Pour into ungreased 9-inch tube pan. Bake 50 minutes. Let cool in pan or on wire rack. Serve plain or with fruit sauce.

Naturally Good Tip: Cakes made with whole-grain flours will be more tender if you replace ¼ cup of each cup flour with cornstarch or arrowroot. (For example, if the recipe calls for 2 cups flour, use 1½ cups flour and ½ cup cornstarch or arrowroot instead.)

CARROT CAKE

Get these ingredients ready:

1 cup raisins
1½ cups water
1½ cups maple syrup
1 tablespoon vanilla *or* 1½ teaspoons almond extract
2 tablespoons oil
2 cups grated carrots
1 teaspoon cinnamon
1 teaspoon nutmeg
1 teaspoon ginger
2¼ cups whole-wheat flour
1 cup chopped walnuts *or* sunflower seeds
2 teaspoons baking powder
1 teaspoon baking soda
1 teaspoon salt

Now follow these steps:

1. Mix raisins, water, maple syrup, vanilla *or* almond extract, oil, carrots, cinnamon, nutmeg, and ginger in a large saucepan.
2. Bring to a boil over high heat; lower to medium and cook for 10 minutes.
3. Pour into a large bowl, cover, and let stand 8–10 hours or overnight.
4. Preheat oven to 275 degrees.
5. Grease and flour a 10-inch tube pan or a 12-cup fluted pan.
6. Mix remaining ingredients into the first mixture with a wooden spoon until the dry ingredients are moistened and everything is well blended. Spoon into prepared baking pan and smooth top with a dull knife or spatula.
7. Bake 1 hour and 45 minutes. Cool on wire rack for 15 minutes. Turn out of pan and finish cooling on serving plate or piece of aluminum foil. Lasts a long time if tightly wrapped.

SECRET INGREDIENT CAKE

Get these ingredients ready:

⅔ cup margarine, softened

1½ cups maple syrup

3 eggs

2 teaspoons vanilla

1¾ cups sifted whole-wheat flour *or* 2 cups sifted unbleached white flour

½ cup carob powder *or* cocoa

1 teaspoon baking soda

1 teaspoon baking powder

½ teaspoon salt

⅔ cup sauerkraut *or* 1 8-ounce can sauerkraut, well drained and chopped or cut into pieces

Now follow these steps:

1. Preheat oven to 350 degrees.
2. Using a large mixing bowl, cream margarine on high speed of electric mixer until fluffy, about 2 minutes.
3. Add maple syrup and beat for 1 minute longer.
4. Beat in one egg for 30 seconds, add another egg and beat 30 seconds, add the last egg and beat 30 seconds more.
5. Stir in the flour, carob powder *or* cocoa, baking soda, baking powder and salt. Using the lowest speed on your mixer, beat until all the dry ingredients are blended in, about 1 minute.
6. Gently fold in the sauerkraut with a wooden spoon or whisk.
7. Grease and flour 2 8-inch round cake pans. Pour equal amounts of batter into each pan.
8. Bake 30 minutes or until cake layers test done when a toothpick or cake tester inserted in the center comes out clean. Remove pans to cooling racks; cool 15 minutes. Turn cakes out of pans onto racks to finish cooling. When cool, frost with Cream Cheese Frosting(page 146)or as desired.

TOFU "CHEESE" CAKE

Get these ingredients ready:

3 eggs
⅔ cup rice syrup *or* ½ cup maple syrup
12 ounces tofu*, crumbled
1 teaspoon vanilla
1 9-inch baked crumb crust(page 141)or pastry pie shell

Now follow these steps:

1. Preheat oven to 375 degrees.
2. Place all ingredients (*except pie shell*) in blender. Blend on high speed for 2 minutes or until very smooth. Pour into pie shell.
3. Bake 35 minutes. Remove from oven and let cool on wire rack. Chill in refrigerator before serving plain or with Strawberry Topping.

STRAWBERRY TOPPING

Get these ingredients ready:

2 tablespoons arrowroot
2 cups strawberries (or other berries)
1 cup apple juice *or* water
¼ cup maple syrup *or* honey
1 tablespoon lemon juice

Now follow these steps:

1. Put arrowroot in a small bowl and slowly stir in ¼ cup of the apple juice or water until smooth.
2. Combine with remaining ingredients (*except lemon juice*) in a small saucepan. Bring mixture to a boil, lower heat and simmer 15 minutes, stirring occasionally. Stir in lemon juice and remove from heat. Refrigerate until cool. Spread on cooled cheesecake.

HAPPY HOLIDAY CAKE

Get these ingredients ready:

1 cup oil
1 cup maple syrup
1 cup honey
2 cups puréed fresh pumpkin *or* canned pumpkin
3 eggs
3 cups sifted whole-wheat flour
2 tablespoons cinnamon
1 teaspoon nutmeg
1 teaspoon salt
1 tablespoon baking powder
2 teaspoons baking soda
2 teaspoons vanilla *or* almond extract
1 cup chopped walnuts *or* pecans
1 cup raisins
½ cup sesame seeds, raw or toasted

Now follow these steps:

1. Preheat oven to 350 degrees.
2. Put oil, maple syrup, honey, pumpkin, and eggs in a large bowl. Beat 2 minutes with electric mixer.
3. Blend flour, cinnamon, nutmeg, and salt into first mixture. Beat 30 seconds with electric mixer.
4. In a small bowl, combine vanilla *or* almond extract, 2 teaspoons water, baking powder, and baking soda. Mix into cake batter and beat for another 30 seconds.
5. Stir in nuts, raisins, and sesame seeds.
6. Spoon into two greased and floured 9-inch cake pans. Bake 50 minutes. Let cool in pans on wire racks. Turn out of pans and frost with Maple Cake Topping(page 145).

PAT-IN-PAN PASTRY

Get these ingredients ready:

1 cup whole-wheat flour
Pinch salt
2 tablespoons sesame seeds *or* finely chopped nuts
⅓ cup oil
2 tablespoons ice water

Now follow these steps:

1. Preheat oven to 450 degrees.
2. Stir together the flour, salt, and sesame seeds *or* nuts, if using, in a medium-size bowl.
3. Stir in oil until mixture looks like a bowl full of small peas.
4. Sprinkle the water over and mix together with a fork until mixture holds together and forms a ball.
5. Put in a 9-inch pie pan and press and pat on bottom and sides of the pan, pressing down with a fork on the rim of the pan. With a dull knife, trim any ragged edges of pastry. Prick holes in the bottom and sides of the pastry with a fork.
6. Bake 15 minutes or until golden brown. Cool and fill.

CRUMB PIE CRUST

Get these ingredients ready:

1 cup very fine, dry bread crumbs
4 tablespoons date sugar *or* 2 tablespoons honey
4 tablespoons oil *or* melted margarine
1 teaspoon cinnamon

Now follow these steps:

1. Mix everything together in a small mixing bowl.
2. Dump into an 8-inch pie pan. Pat evenly on the bottom and sides of the pan.
3. Chill for at least ½ hour *or* bake for 15 minutes in a 325 degree oven before filling.

"CHEESE" PASTRY

Get these ingredients ready:

> 1 cup margarine *or* ½ cup margarine and ⅓ cup oil
> 1 cup tofu*, crumbled and well drained
> 2 cups sifted whole-wheat flour
> 1 tablespoon honey
> ¼ teaspoon salt

Now follow these steps:

1. Cream margarine, honey, and tofu together until smooth and creamy.
2. Sift together remaining ingredients. Work into creamed mixture with a pastry cutter or wooden spoon until completely blended in.
3. Form into a ball; wrap in plastic wrap and chill several hours.
4. Using a well floured board or pastry cloth and rolling pin, roll out to about ⅛-inch thick. Use as directed for pie shell or to make Jim Jams.

JIM JAMS

Get these ingredients ready:

> 1 recipe "Cheese" Pastry
> Cherry *or* raspberry jam *or* preserves

Now follow these steps:

1. Preheat oven to 425 degrees.
2. Roll pastry ⅛-inch thick; cut into 2½-inch squares. Place a teaspoonful of jam or preserves in the center of each square. Fold corners to the center to enclose filling. Place on cookie sheets.
3. Bake 15 minutes. Cool. Just like mini Pop-Tarts and nutritious enough to serve for breakfast.

COCONUT PECAN PIE

Get these ingredients ready:

1 8- or 9-inch unbaked pie shell
1 cup chopped pecans
1 cup unsweetened coconut
1¼ cups maple syrup
¼ teaspoon salt
6 tablespoons oil *or* melted margarine
3 eggs

Now follow these steps:

1. Preheat oven to 400 degrees.
2. Sprinkle nuts in bottom of pie shell.
3. Sprinkle coconut over nuts.
4. Mix remaining ingredients together well with wooden spoon or electric mixer and pour into pie shell.
5. Bake 15 minutes at 400 degrees, then lower the oven temperature to 350 degrees and bake for another 25 minutes. Cool before eating.

Naturally Good Tip: Measure the oil called for in your recipe first; when you measure the sweetener (in the same cup), it will slide right out.

PUMPKIN PIE

Get these ingredients ready:

1¾ cups puréed fresh pumpkin *or* canned pumpkin
2 eggs
½ teaspoon salt
1 teaspoon cinnamon
½ teaspoon ginger
¼ teaspoon nutmeg
1 cup maple syrup
1 cup squash "milk" (page 55) *or* soy milk
1 9- or 10-inch unbaked pie shell

Now follow these steps:

1. Preheat oven to 425 degrees.
2. Bake pie shell 5 minutes. Remove from oven and let cool while you make filling.
3. Place all remaining ingredients in blender and blend until very smooth, about 1 minute. Pour into cooled pie shell.
4. Bake 15 minutes. Lower oven temperature to 350 degrees and continue baking 45 minutes. Remove and let cool before eating. To store, keep covered in refrigerator.

MAPLE CAKE TOPPING

Get these ingredients ready:

½ cup peanut *or* almond butter
½ cup margarine
½ cup maple syrup

Now follow these steps:

1. Combine nut butter and margarine in a small bowl. Beat until soft and creamy with an electric mixer or wooden spoon.
2. Keep the mixer or spoon going and slowly pour in the maple syrup. Beat until fluffy. Spread on top of an 8- or 9-inch square cake (or just plop it on with a spoon).

SWEET FRUIT GLAZE

Get these ingredients ready:

2 tablespoons plus 1 cup fruit juice (apple or pear is good)
1 tablespoon arrowroot*
Pinch of salt
¼ cup sesame seeds *or* chopped nuts (optional)

Now follow these steps:

1. In a small bowl, mix the arrowroot and the 2 tablespoons juice until smooth.
2. Bring the 1 cup juice and the salt to a boil in a small saucepan.
3. Slowly pour the arrowroot-juice mixture into the boiling juice, stirring constantly.
4. Cook and stir until thick and clear, about 1 minute.
5. Pour over cake or cookies right away. Sprinkle with seeds or nuts.

CREAM CHEESE FROSTING

Get these ingredients ready:

8-ounces cream cheese
1 cup tofu*, crumbled and well drained
¼ – ½ cup honey
Pinch salt
½ cup carob powder *or* cocoa (optional)

Now follow these steps:

1. Put all ingredients in a medium-size mixing bowl.
2. Beat with an electric mixer until creamy, about 3 minutes.

TOFU WHIP

Get these ingredients ready:

1 cup crumbled tofu*, well drained
2 tablespoons maple syrup, rice syrup*, *or* honey
½ teaspoon vanilla
½ cup chopped fruit† (optional)

Now follow these steps:

1. Place all ingredients in blender and blend on high for 1–1½ minutes or until smooth and creamy. Spread or spoon on cakes or desserts.

†Fresh strawberries, bananas, peaches, or persimmons.

FLUFFY SNOW ICING

Get these ingredients ready:

2 cups maple syrup
2 egg whites
Pinch salt

Now follow these steps:

1. Put the maple syrup in a heavy, medium-size saucepan.
2. Cook over medium heat, stirring occasionally, until temperature is 232°F. on a candy thermometer.
3. Meanwhile, put egg whites into a large glass mixing bowl and get your electric mixer out and ready to go.
4. When maple syrup has reached the required temperature, take the saucepan (very carefully, using a pot holder) and begin to pour the syrup, very slowly, into the egg whites. *At the same time,* beat the egg whites at high speed with the electric mixer. Keep on pouring and beating until all the syrup is in and the icing is as thick as you like, about 5 to 7 minutes.

Naturally Good Tip: Here's a super easy frosting. When cupcakes or cookies are baked, remove from oven and place on cooling rack. Sprinkle ½-dozen carob chips on each one. Cover with a piece of aluminum foil and let stand a minute until the chips soften. Remove the foil and spread the chips with a dull knife. Cool.

Fillers and Fancies

Did you turn to this section first?

That's o.k. Even snacks and munchies can contribute to your well-being. Nuts, for example, are one of the most concentrated sources of minerals and fatty acids. Popcorn supplies fiber and phosphorus for very few calories (if served plain, of course). Even dips and chips can motivate your muscles when they are made from tofu and whole grains.

Besides, they are the quickest solution for that empty space in your stomach. And this is an ideal time to experiment in the kitchen. (You can take chances on inventing all sorts of concoctions if you know you'll be getting a *real* meal later.)

So take the plunge! Just remember to save some sesame seeds for dinner!

TORTILLA CHIPS

Get these ingredients ready:

    6 corn tortillas
    ¼ teaspoon salt

Now follow these steps:

1. Preheat oven to 400 degrees.
2. Cut each tortilla into 5 or 6 pie-shaped wedges.
3. Place wedges on an ungreased cookie sheet and sprinkle evenly with the salt.
4. Bake 10 minutes. Turn over with a spatula and bake 2–3 minutes longer.
5. Cool slightly on wire racks or paper towels. Enjoy plain or serve with Onion Dip.

ONION DIP

Get these ingredients ready:

    2 onions
    2 cloves garlic (optional)
    3 tablespoons oil
    1 tablespoon tamari sauce*
    1 tablespoon lemon juice
    ½ teaspoon salt
    2 cups drained and crumbled tofu*

Now follow these steps:

1. Peel and thinly slice the onions and garlic. Sauté in the oil in a frying pan until clear and beginning to brown, about 10–15 minutes.
2. Put half the onion mixture, remaining ingredients, and 1 cup of the tofu in blender. Blend at high speed until very smooth. Repeat with remaining onion mixture and tofu. Mix both batches together in a serving bowl. Refrigerate at least 2 hours before serving. Good with tortilla chips, pita bread and chopped vegetables, cooked grains, or almost anything!

TOFU DIP

Get these ingredients ready:

1 onion, chopped
½ cup oil
2 tablespoons lemon juice
1½ cups crumbled tofu*, drained
2 teaspoons maple syrup
2 umeboshi plums*, pitted and mashed (optional)
1 teaspoon prepared mustard
1 teaspoon tamari sauce* *or* ¼ teaspoon salt

Now follow these steps:

1. Sauté the onion in the oil in a small frying pan for 10 minutes.
2. Put onion and all other ingredients in blender. Blend until smooth, about 1 minute.
3. Chill at least 1 hour before serving.

CLAM ZIPPEDY DIP

Get these ingredients ready:

1 8-ounce can minced clams
1 3-ounce package cream cheese
1 cup crumbled tofu*
3 tablespoons lemon juice
1 small onion, minced
2 tablespoons tomato sauce *or* catsup
1 tablespoon tamari sauce*

Now follow these steps:

1. Drain juice from clams into blender. (Set clams aside.) Add remaining ingredients to clam juice. Blend 1 minute at high speed or until smooth and creamy. Pour into serving bowl.
2. Stir in clams. Serve on crackers, corn chips, or vegetable sticks.

NUT BUTTER TOFU SPREAD

Get these ingredients ready:

    1 cup drained and crumbled tofu*
    1 cup nut butter
    1 tablespoon maple syrup *or* honey
    1 tablespoon miso* (optional)
    ½ cup chopped dried fruit *or* raisins

Now follow these steps:

1. Mix everything together with a fork in a small bowl.
2. Cover and store in refrigerator. Good on crackers.

BANANA POPS

Get these ingredients ready:

    3 ripe bananas
    1 cup carob chips*
    1 tablespoon maple syrup
    4 teaspoons margarine
    1 cup finely chopped nuts
    6 sticks (optional)

Now follow these steps:

1. Peel bananas and cut them in half crosswise.
2. Combine the carob chips, maple syrup, and margarine in a small saucepan. Place over low heat and cook, stirring constantly, until chips and margarine are melted.
3. With clean hands or a dull knife, pat or spread the mixture on the bananas, trying to cover them completely.
4. Place the chopped nuts on a plate or piece of waxed paper and roll the bananas in them until covered. Push a stick (if using) into the flat end of each banana half.
5. Carefully place each banana pop in a small plastic or waxed paper bag and freeze until hardened.

CHEERS TO GOOD DRINKS

Nutritious Nutshake

½ cup raw cashew pieces
1 cup water *or* apple juice
2 bananas *or* very ripe peaches, peeled and sliced or cut up
1 teaspoon vanilla

Put nuts and water or apple juice in blender and blend for 2 minutes. Add the remaining ingredients and blend 1 minute longer at high speed.

Strawberry Banana Shake

2 cups dairy milk *or* substitute milk (page 55)
1–2 cups sliced fresh strawberries
1 banana, sliced
¼ teaspoon vanilla *or* almond extract

Put all ingredients in blender and blend on high speed until smooth.

Peachy Keen Shake

2 cups dairy milk *or* substitute milk (page 55)
2 peaches, peeled and sliced
½ teaspoon cinnamon *or* almond extract
½ cup crumbled tofu* (optional)

Put all ingredients in blender and blend on high speed until smooth.

Creamy Carob Shake

2 tablespoons carob syrup (page 161)
¼ cup nut butter (peanut, almond, or cashew)
1½ cups dairy milk *or* substitute milk (page 55)
½ teaspoon vanilla

Put all ingredients in blender and blend on high speed until smooth.

DRINKS FOR A COLD DAY

A Cuppa Cocoa

>4 teaspoons cocoa
>1 tablespoon honey
>1 tablespoon maple syrup
>1 tablespoon water
>¾ cup dairy milk *or* substitute milk (page 55)

Mix cocoa, honey, maple syrup, and water together in your favorite hot cocoa cup, until very smooth. Heat the milk in a small saucepan, over low heat, until it is hot but not boiling. Pour the hot milk into your cup with the cocoa mixture and stir well.

And a Cuppa Carob

>1 tablespoon carob powder*
>2 tablespoons maple syrup
>¼ cup tofu, crumbled
>¾ cup hot water

Put all ingredients in blender and blend on high speed for 1 minute. Pour into small saucepan and heat until hot but not boiling.

Kuchicha Tea

>1 teaspoon kuchicha tea (from the natural foods store)
>1 cup of water

Combine the tea and water in a small saucepan. Bring to a boil over high heat. Reduce heat and simmer for 15 minutes. Strain through a fine mesh strainer into cup. Enjoy plain or with lemon juice and honey, maple syrup, or rice syrup. To make Kuchicha Soy Sizzle, stir in 1 teaspoon tamari sauce* instead of lemon and sweetener. It will warm even the coldest bones!

White Lightning

> 1 cup boiling (or very hot) water
> 1–2 teaspoons honey *or* maple syrup
> 2–3 teaspoons lemon juice

Stir all ingredients together in a cup and drink while hot. Good anytime but especially when you have a cold.

Hot 'n' Spicy Apple Drink

> 1 cup apple cider *or* apple juice
> 1 stick cinnamon
> 1–2 whole cloves

Put ingredients in small saucepan and heat over low heat until hot but not boiling. Strain through fine mesh strainer into cup.

CRANBERRY JUICE

Get these ingredients ready:

> 2 cups fresh or frozen cranberries
> 2 cups water
> ½ cup maple syrup *or* ¼ cup honey
> 1 tablespoon lemon juice (optional)

Now follow these steps:

1. Put the cranberries and water in a medium-size saucepan. Bring to boil and simmer for 5–7 minutes, on medium heat, until the cranberries "pop" and the skins split.
2. Strain through a fine mesh strainer into a small saucepan. Stir in the maple syrup *or* honey.
3. Bring the sweetened cranberry juice to a boil over medium heat. Lower heat and simmer for 2 to 3 minutes.
4. Chill in refrigerator. Stir in lemon juice before drinking, if desired.

MAPLE NUT POPCORN BALLS

Get these ingredients ready:

2 cups maple syrup
10 cups freshly popped popcorn
¾ cup chopped nuts
2 tablespoons almond extract (optional)
2 tablespoons margarine *or* oil

Now follow these steps:

1. Put syrup in a medium-size heavy saucepan over medium-low heat. Insert candy thermometer and cook syrup until temperature reaches 260 degrees. (This may take 30–40 minutes but start checking the temperature after 20 minutes.)
2. Meanwhile, combine the popcorn and nuts in a large bowl.
3. When temperature is reached, remove syrup from heat and stir in the margarine *or* oil and almond extract. Pour evenly over the popcorn and nuts, stirring to mix well.
4. Grease your hands and form the mixture into about 10 balls.
5. Eat right away or wrap each ball in waxed paper or plastic wrap to store.

PEANUT SUNFLOWER SNAPS

Get these ingredients ready:

½ cup peanut butter
¼ cup honey
½ cup sunflower seeds
½ cup currants
½ cup chopped apricots
1½ cups unsweetened coconut

Now follow these steps:

1. Mix all ingredients together in a medium-size bowl using your hands. Mix until ingredients stick together.
2. With greased hands, form 1-inch balls and place on waxed paper or cookie sheets. Let stand, at room temperature, for 3–4 hours or until they are firm and slightly dry. Store in a glass jar or other covered container in the refrigerator.

ALMOND SESAME CRACKLE

Get these ingredients ready:

½ cup maple syrup
⅓ cup oil
½ teaspoon almond *or* vanilla extract
1 cup chopped almonds
1 cup sesame seeds
½ cup rolled rye *or* oats
2 tablespoons whole-wheat flour

Now follow these steps:

1. Preheat oven to 350 degrees.
2. Put all ingredients in a large mixing bowl. Mix with a wooden spoon until well combined.
3. Spread the mixture evenly in a greased 9″ × 13″ baking pan. Smooth with wet hands or dull knife.
4. Bake 20 minutes. Cool in pan on wire rack. When cool, cut into squares.

CRUNCHY FRUIT MUNCH

Get these ingredients ready:

> 3 quarts freshly popped Jolly Time Pop Corn
> 2 cups natural cereal with raisins
> ¾ cup dried apricots, chopped
> ¼ teaspoon salt
> ⅓ cup butter *or* margarine
> ¼ cup honey

Now follow these steps:

1. Preheat oven to 300 degrees.
2. Combine first four ingredients in large baking pan. Set aside.
3. In small saucepan, combine butter *or* margarine and honey. Cook over low heat until butter *or* margarine is melted. Pour over pop corn mixture, tossing lightly until well coated.
4. Place in oven. Bake 30 minutes, stirring occasionally. Makes 3 quarts. Store in tightly covered container up to 2 weeks.

Naturally Good Tip: This recipe is reprinted by permission of the people at the American Pop Corn Company who make Jolly Time Pop Corn. They will send you a recipe folder filled with nutritious snack recipes if you write to them and send 25¢ for postage and handling to: American Pop Corn Company, P.O. Box 178, Sioux City, IA 51102. Don't forget to include your complete address and ZIP.

CAROB RAISIN 'N' NUTS

Get these ingredients ready:

¼ pound unsweetened carob chips
⅓ cup maple syrup *or* ½ cup rice syrup
1 teaspoon vanilla
1½ cups raisins *or* nuts

Now follow these steps:

1. In a medium-size saucepan over low heat, melt carob chips, stirring constantly.
2. Stir in maple syrup *or* rice syrup. Remove from heat and let cool to room temperature.
3. Stir in vanilla and beat well with a wooden spoon for about 1 minute.
4. Mix in raisins or nuts. Drop by tablespoonfuls onto waxed paper or lightly greased cookie sheets. When firm, remove and store, covered, in the refrigerator.

CANDY CRISPS

Get these ingredients ready:

1 cup maple syrup
¾ cup peanut, almond *or* cashew butter
4 cups Puffed Brown Rice *or* Nutri-Grain Flaked Cereal
1 cup chopped nuts

Now follow these steps:

1. Grease a 9″ × 13″ pan.
2. Boil maple syrup for 2 minutes. Remove from heat and stir in the nut butter until well blended. Pour into prepared pan.
3. Sprinkle the cereal and nuts on top of the syrup-nut butter mixture and mix until evenly blended. Press into a smooth layer with clean, wet hands. Allow to cool. Cut into squares. Store, covered, in a cool place or in refrigerator.

NUTS TO YOU!

Plain Toasted Nuts

> 1–4 cups whole or chopped nuts

Preheat oven to 350 degrees. Spread nuts evenly on cookie sheet(s). Bake 10 minutes, stirring the nuts after 5 minutes. Remove from oven and cool before munching or adding to a recipe.

Plain Roasted Nuts

Follow the directions for Plain Toasted Nuts except grease each cookie sheet with 1 tablespoon oil before baking.

Tamari Roasted Nuts

> 2 cups whole or chopped nuts
> 1 tablespoon tamari sauce*
> 1 tablespoon oil

Combine the nuts and tamari sauce in a small bowl. Grease cookie sheet and follow directions for Plain Toasted Nuts.

Crunchy Nuts

> 2 cups chopped nuts
> 2 tablespoons sesame seeds
> ½ teaspoon salt
> 2 tablespoons sesame oil

Combine ingredients, spread on cookie sheet and follow the directions for Plain Toasted Nuts.

So Sweet Nuts

> 1 cup whole almonds
> 2 tablespoons soft margarine *or* oil
> ½ cup maple syrup

Combine ingredients, spread on cookie sheet and follow the directions for Plain Toasted Nuts. (These may take a few minutes longer but check them occasionally because they burn more easily than the others.) Let cool and break apart if stuck together.

CAROB SYRUP

Get these ingredients ready:

½ cup carob powder* *or* cocoa
¾ cup water
1¼ cups maple syrup
Dash salt
½ teaspoon vanilla

Now follow these steps:

1. Combine carob powder *or* cocoa, water, maple syrup, and salt in small saucepan.
2. Bring to boil over medium heat, stirring occasionally, and simmer 5 minutes or until ingredients are blended. Add vanilla.

BLUEBERRY SAUCE

Get these ingredients ready:

2 cups fresh blueberries
1 cup water
3 tablespoons maple syrup
2 tablespoons cornstarch
2 tablespoons lemon juice

Now follow these steps:

1. Mix blueberries, water, and maple syrup together in medium-size saucepan.
2. In a small dish, mix together the cornstarch and lemon juice until smooth.
3. Bring blueberry-water-syrup mixture to boiling over medium heat, stirring constantly. Slowly stir in the cornstarch-lemon mixture. Cook and stir 1 minute.
4. Remove from heat and let cool slightly. Wonderful on pancakes; good on cakes and puddings, too.

DESSERT SAUCE

Get these ingredients ready:

2 teaspoons arrowroot *or* kuzu*
1 cup water
½ cup maple syrup *or* rice syrup*
2 tablespoons margarine *or* oil
2 tablespoons tahini *or* cashew butter
1½ teaspoon vanilla
½ cup roasted chopped nuts (page 160)

Now follow these steps:

1. Put arrowroot *or* kuzu in small saucepan. Slowly stir in water until mixture is free of lumps. Stir in the maple syrup *or* rice syrup.
2. Bring mixture to a boil over medium heat, stirring constantly. Cook and stir for 1 minute.
3. Remove pan from heat and stir in remaining ingredients. Serve hot, warm, or cool over cakes, stewed fruit, or puddings.

Naturally Good Tip: Popcorn won't pop? Either place the popcorn in the freezer for a couple of hours or put the amount you need in a mesh strainer and hold under running water until all the kernels are wet. Shake off the excess water and pop according to directions on the package.

MUSTARD SAUCE

Get these ingredients ready:

 ⅓ cup crumbled tofu*
 ⅔ cup water
 3 tablespoons mayonnaise *or* Tofu Mayonnaise (page 164)
 1½ tablespoons prepared mustard
 ¼ teaspoon salt
 1 tablespoon oil
 2 tablespoons unbleached white flour

Now follow these steps:

1. Put the tofu, water, mayonnaise, mustard, and salt in blender and whiz until smooth.
2. Put the oil in a small saucepan and stir in the flour until a smooth paste forms. Cook and stir over medium heat for 2 minutes. Remove from heat.
3. Slowly stir in the blended mixture. Return to heat and cook and stir until as thick as you like. Remove from heat and stir in lemon juice. Serve over vegetables.

NUTTY ALMOND SAUCE

Get these ingredients ready:

    1 large onion, minced
    1 tablespoon oil
    ¾ cup vegetable broth *or* water
    ¼ teaspoon salt
    ½ cup almond butter
    ½ cup chopped roasted almonds (page 160)

Now follow these steps:

1. Sauté onion in oil in a small frying pan for 5 minutes on medium-high heat.
2. Remove from heat and stir in almond butter. Slowly stir in broth *or* water until smooth.
3. Bring to a boil over high heat, stirring constantly. Lower heat and cook 5 minutes, stirring often.
4. Stir in salt and almonds. Serve over grains, vegetables, or noodles.

TOFU MAYONNAISE

Get these ingredients ready:

    ½ cup oil
    ¼ cup cider vinegar *or* rice vinegar
    2 cloves garlic, chopped
    1 cup crumbled tofu*

Now follow these steps:

1. Put all ingredients in blender and whiz on high speed until very smooth, 1–2 minutes. Chill. Stays fresh about 4–5 days if covered and refrigerated.

CUCUMBER-DILL DRESSING

Get these ingredients ready:

    1 cup soft, crumbled tofu*
    1 cup chopped cucumber, seeds removed
    1 tablespoon cider vinegar *or* rice vinegar
    ¼ teaspoon salt
    1 teaspoon dried dillweed *or* 1 tablespoon fresh dill
    1 teaspoon oil (optional)
    1 teaspoon lemon juice (optional)

Now follow these steps:

1. Put all ingredients in blender. Whiz on high speed until smooth, about 1 minute.
2. Serve on tossed green salad or cold cooked vegetables.

ITALIAN SALAD DRESSING

Get these ingredients ready:

    ¼ cup oil
    ½ cup cider vinegar *or* lemon juice
    2–3 tablespoons apple juice
    ½ teaspoon oregano
    1 teaspoon prepared mustard
    ½ teaspoon celery seeds
    ½ teaspoon paprika
    ¼ teaspoon thyme
    1 clove garlic, minced (optional)
    2 tablespoons minced onion (optional)

Now follow these steps:

1. Put everything in blender and whiz 30 seconds or put in a tightly covered jar and shake until well mixed.

PICKLED CUCUMBER ROUNDS

Get these ingredients ready:

>   5 cucumbers, unwaxed and well scrubbed but not peeled
>   2 cups apple cider vinegar
>   1-inch thick slice of gingerroot*
>   1 tablespoon mustard seeds
>   1 tablespoon whole allspice
>   1 tablespoon whole cloves
>   1 tablespoon whole peppercorns (optional)
>   2 cups maple syrup

Now follow these steps:

1. Cut cucumbers into ¼-inch thick slices.
2. Put all remaining ingredients in medium-size saucepan. Bring to boil and boil, uncovered, 5 minutes.
3. Divide the cucumber slices evenly between two 1 quart canning jars.
4. Pour the hot liquid over the cucumbers in each jar, covering them completely. Screw the jar tops on tightly. Store in refrigerator. Turn upside down (and back again) once or twice a day for 4–5 days. Then, eat 'em up!

SWEET AND SOUR CUCUMBERS

Get these ingredients ready:

2 cups apple cider vinegar
2 cloves garlic, minced
1-inch thick slice of gingerroot*
1 tablespoon celery seeds
1 tablespoon whole cloves
1 tablespoon allspice
1 tablespoon peppercorns
2 cups maple syrup
5 medium-size cucumbers

Now follow these steps:

1. Put all ingredients, except the cucumbers, in a medium-size saucepan. Bring to a boil over medium heat and boil, uncovered, for 5 minutes.
2. Cool to room temperature.
3. Meanwhile, cut the cucumbers into ¼-inch thick slices. Divide the slices equally between two 1 quart canning jars.
4. When cool, strain the vinegar-syrup mixture. Pour over cucumbers in jars until jars are filled to overflowing. Screw the lids on very tightly and wipe the outsides of the jars clean. Store in refrigerator for 4–5 days before eating. While you are waiting, turn the jars over (and back again) once or twice a day.

Food Dictionary

Agar (also called kanten) is a gelatin made from seaweed and is used to thicken. Contains some iron, iodine, and other nutrients.

Almond butter is similar to peanut butter. Made from raw or roasted almonds, it is available at natural food stores. Almonds are a good source of oil soluble nutrients, including linoleic acid.

Arame is a dried and shredded sea vegetable.

Arrowroot is a starch made from powdered arrowroot and can be used instead of flour for thickening. (Kuzu can be used interchangeably with arrowroot.) Find both in natural food and some grocery stores.

Barley is a mild flavored grain which can be used in any recipe calling for rice. It comes as a hulled whole grain (try for this type) or pearled in natural food and grocery stores.

Barley Malt is a syrup made from germinated barley and is used for sweetening.

Bran is the part of the wheat hull that is left after whole-wheat has been ground into flour and sifted. It provides fiber and gives a crunchy texture to foods.

Bulgur is cracked and parched whole-wheat. High in nutrients, easy and fast to cook, bulgur is a good addition to your kitchen. Found in natural food and most grocery stores.

Carob comes as a powder, similar to cocoa in appearance but higher in nutrients and lower in fat. Cocoa can be substituted. Found in natural food stores.

Cashew butter is used like peanut butter and is available made from raw or roasted cashews.

Coconut is at its flavorful best when it is freshly grated. If you use dried coconut, be sure to get the unsweetened flakes or shreds that have not been treated with chemical preservatives.

Cornmeal is ground from dried corn. Get the coarse kind that has not been degerminated. (Yellow cornmeal has more vitamin A than white cornmeal.)

Date sugar is made from ground, dried dates. If you like dates, you'll enjoy date sugar. (Try it hot on cereals.) Available in some natural food stores.

Dried corn (not popping corn) is made from—you guessed it—kernels of fresh corn that are dried. Soak them overnight before cooking. Found at natural food stores.

Dulse is a red sea vegetable which is dried in sheets and flaked or powdered. Very nutritious and one of the tastiest to people unaccustomed to sea vegetables. Find in natural food stores.

Egg roll wrappers are like thin pancakes that are used to enclose a filling and then are fried as are egg rolls or won-tons. You'll find them in the freezer case or fresh vegetable section of your natural food store or supermarket.

Fruit is often available dried. Look for the unsulfured kind at natural food stores.

Gingerroot is a root used in oriental cooking from which dried, powdered ginger is made. Find the fresh root in natural food and grocery stores. If not using within a few days, keep it wrapped in foil in the freezer and simply grate off the desired amount as you need it.

Hijiki is a dried sea vegetable with large amounts of calcium, protein, and minerals.

Honey is a natural sweetener made when bees drink and digest flower nectar. It is a natural form of sugar which is easily converted for use by the body.

Kelp is a dried sea vegetable rich in vitamins and minerals. Often used powdered in place of salt. Find in natural food stores.

Lentils are among the most nutritious of the dried beans. They come in green or red varieties and are tasty and easily cooked. Find in natural food or grocery stores.

Maple syrup is a natural sweetener containing iron, calcium, and other nutrients. Get the 100% pure maple syrup that has not been processed with formaldehyde and which contains no added sugar, corn syrup, coloring or preservatives. (These are usually Canadian brands since the use of formaldehyde is prohibited in Canada.)

Millet is a delicious, small whole grain which can be used in any recipe calling for rice.

Miso is a fermented paste made from soybeans (and sometimes grains) that is used as a seasoning. It contains protein and vitamin B_{12}.

Nori is a dried sea vegetable high in protein and vitamin A.

Oatmeal is the flakes of oats to which we are all accustomed. Try steel cut oatmeal too.

Peanut butter called for in these recipes is always the unhydrogenated kind without additives. Find it at natural food and grocery stores.

Rice called for in these recipes is always brown rice. (I prefer organic short grain rice.) Get at natural food and some grocery stores.

Rice syrup is a pure, natural sweetener made from rice, water, malted barley, and enzymes from malted grain. Use it for cooking or on pancakes. Find in natural food stores.

Rolled rye is similar in appearance to oatmeal and can be used in the same ways. Find in natural food stores.

Sea Salt, the only salt called for in these recipes, is made from dehydrated sea water and contains trace minerals.

Sesame seeds are very nutritious and mild in flavor. Try to find the black (unhulled) sesame seeds which are higher in calcium. Find in natural food and some grocery stores.

Shoyu is soy sauce made from fermented soybeans and wheat. Used as a seasoning. Find in natural food and grocery stores.

Soybeans are versatile, dried beans that can be used cooked, or made into soy milk, soy sauce, tofu, tempeh, and miso. They are the only vegetable that contains all the essential amino acids, as well as many minerals and vitamins. Find in natural food or grocery stores.

Soy grits are little chunks made from cracked toasted soybeans or from soy flour. Can be added to casseroles, cereals and breads for extra nutrition.

Sunflower seeds are very rich in nutrients and can be eaten raw or roasted and used in place of nuts in baking. Found in natural food and most grocery stores.

Tamari is a soy sauce made purely from fermented soybeans with nothing added. A wonderful seasoning, it is available in natural food stores.

Tahini is a seed butter made from ground sesame seeds which can be used in cooking and baking or as a dip or sandwich spread. Found in natural food and some grocery stores.

Tapioca is made from the root of the cassava plant and is often used in pudding or as a thickener. Comes whole and pearled. Find in natural food or grocery stores.

Tofu is a white creamy cheeselike curd made from soybeans. Contains all 8 essential amino acids, minerals, and vitamins.

Vanilla called for in these recipes is pure vanilla extract and is found anywhere.

Wakame is a dried sea vegetable rich in protein and minerals. Makes a flavorful addition to soups. Find in natural food and oriental grocery stores.

Wheat germ is the inner part of the wheat kernel. Very nutritious, it is available raw or toasted. Found in natural food or grocery stores.

Whole-wheat berries are the grain of whole wheat. Can be eaten cooked or sprouted. Find them at natural food stores.

Yogurt is a custardlike food made from fermented dairy milk or soy milk. Use for baking or in desserts, toppings, or dips. Look for the unsweetened, unflavored kind in natural food or grocery stores.

Index

Recipe Index

General Index